"We Want to Be Known"

"We Want to Be Known"

Learning from Adolescent Girls

Edited by

Ruth Shagoury Hubbard, Maureen Barbieri,

and Brenda Miller Power

STENHOUSE PUBLISHERS
York, Maine

Stenhouse Publishers, 431 York Street, York, Maine 03909
www.stenhouse.com

Credits
Chapter 7: Portions of this chapter originally appeared in *Feisty Females: Inspiring Girls to Think Mathematically* by Karen Karp, E. Todd Brown, Linda Allen, and Candy Allen (Heinemann, a division of Reed Elsevier Inc., Portsmouth, NH, 1998).

Library of Congress Cataloging-in-Publication Data
We want to be known : learning from adolescent girls / edited by Ruth Shagoury Hubbard, Maureen Barbieri, and Brenda Miller Power.
p. cm.
Includes bibliographical references.
ISBN 1-57110-079-2
1. Teenage girls—Education—United States. 2. Teenage girls—United States—Attitudes. 3. Adolescent psychology—United States. 4. Interpersonal communication in adolescence—United States. 5. Women—Socialization—United States. 6. Sex role—United States. I. Hubbard, Ruth, 1950– . II. Barbieri, Maureen. III. Power, Brenda Miller.
HQ798.W3 1998
305.235—dc21 98-17021
CIP

Cover and interior design by Ron Kosciak, *Dragonfly Design*
Cover illustration by Julia
Typeset by Achorn Graphics

Manufactured in the United States of America on acid-free paper
03 02 01 00 99 98 9 8 7 6 5 4 3 2 1

For our wise and understanding daughters:

Meghan Hubbard,

Erin Blahut,

and Deanna Power

Contents

The pieces in italics are essays or poems written by teenage girls about the adolescent experience.

Acknowledgments

Our first thanks go to the contributors, who carved time out of their busy professional lives to work on their chapters. From beginning teachers to veterans, the authors in this collection are stretching us in our thinking of what's possible in the schools for girls, and for boys. We are grateful for their insights, their commitment to their students, and their willingness to share their classroom stories with a wider audience. (Not to mention their good humor in deadlines that always seemed to fall when a school crisis was erupting.)

We are fortunate to have the voices of many adolescent girls woven throughout this book. Their enthusiasm for writing essays and book recommendations for their younger sisters is inspiring. Special thanks to their teachers, especially Linda Christensen, Tim Gillespie, and Sharon Frye for setting in motion "action plans" that encouraged the young women in their classes to take their work beyond the classroom walls. We also wish to thank the many girls who educated us about what is going on in their lives, meeting with us during and after school to explain their world from their point of view. Danling Fu, friend and colleague, inspired our title. Thanks, Danling!

We are deeply appreciative of the support and encouragement of our friend and editor Philippa Stratton. She has been instrumental in shaping the book, offering suggestions and wise counsel—and very funny e-mail messages at the moments when they were most needed.

Support from our families has sustained us. A special thanks to Nathan Hubbard for the hours he spent tracking down references on the Internet for our resource section. Nathan, you're a lifesaver!

1

Going to the Well: Learning from Girls and Their Teachers

In Eve Merriam's book *The Wise Woman and Her Secret* (1991), a group of rural townspeople hike out to the cabin of an old woman who is rumored to have the secret of knowledge and happiness. After badgering the woman and searching her land for the "secret," the crowd is disgruntled when they find nothing. All leave, save for one young girl.

The girl shows the wise woman a penny she has found in a well. After the girl marvels about the color of the penny, examines its texture, and speculates about where it came from, the wise woman exclaims in delight that the girl has discovered the secret of wisdom: to be curious, to look closely at small things around you in the world, and to want to learn more.

Sometimes, in searching for wisdom about working with and understanding girls, educators can be as blind as those townspeople. We frantically try to define gender issues in understandable terms, and just as quickly to come up with solutions to these problems. We discover girls aren't called on enough in class; we call on them more. We decide the media promotes negative body images for girls, and rid our classrooms of *Seventeen* magazine.

But the truth of who young girls are, and what we could help them become, is often more complicated than the research suggests. What's missing in much of the gender research is the strong voice of teachers who work closely with girls, who help them on a daily basis deal with what it means to be a strong female. Often research on gender is based on survey information, or on the perspective of outside researchers looking in at classroom practice. It's understandable that we might crave a distant voice of authority when it comes to gender issues. What's hard to face in dealing with girls who are entering adolescence often is what's hard to deal with in ourselves—the patterns of language, power, and hidden agendas can be almost impossible for us to see clearly, let alone change.

That's why this collection of essays has been such a joy for us to read and edit. The contributors to "*We Want to Be Known*" observe, delight in, and struggle with the everyday routines and rituals girls go through as they become teenagers. The authors of this book are wise—they know the secret in learning to work with girls is to be curious. They are not afraid to slow down, look closely, and ask tough questions about what it means to be a girl entering adolescence in American classrooms today. The questions they pose defy easy analysis: Why do some girls talk more than others? What happens when all-girl social groups are directed by strong female teachers? How can older teens mentor younger peers? How does culture affect gender roles in second language learners?

These essays from classroom teachers are framed by contributions from girls. In narratives and poems, these young women show they have much to teach us about their needs. Wisdom starts at a very early age—especially when it involves sorting out what growing up female might mean.

Those who think they understand the needs of girls will be challenged by this collection. Just calling on girls more or working to rid the classroom of passive female stereotypes won't transform the gender dynamics of our classrooms. It's not only a girl thing—it's a learning thing. If we can know girls better, we can know ourselves in new ways. Gender matters. It does make a difference in how, what, and even if girls learn in schools. If we can acknowledge this, we will be best able to change our classrooms, teaching styles and lessons to help all students realize their potential.

Reference

Merriam, Eve. 1991. *The Wise Woman and Her Secret*. New York: Simon & Schuster.

Gurl

Mary Blalock

From Adam's rib
it's prophesied
I came,
but that's his story.

I'm walking on my own

down these streets
with a stop sign on every
corner,
takin' my time.
I've got no place to go 'cept
forward.

Down these highways without
a road map,
down these sidewalks,
where the cracks want to

break my mother's back,
where the city is crowded.

I'm walking on my own.

I'm not on a Stairmaster,
and I won't wait for an elevator.
I'm taking the fire escape
to the top floor.

If I want to,
I'll walk all around the world,
taking the long way
or the shortcuts,
'cross countries and through
oceans.
I won't be swimming.
I'll walk
on my own.

2

Revisiting Adolescence

Ellena Weldon

ADOLESCENCE. Those awkward transition years of middle school and high school. Some of us might purposefully erase memories of this time from our consciousness, but as a female adult teacher of teenaged children, I cannot forget. I am immersed in adolescence every day. In order for me to see the world through my students' eyes, I believe it is important to remember what my life was like at that age. What classes did I enjoy and why? Who were my most influential teachers? Who did I want to emulate in my own teaching? How did I feel about myself? What questions did I have that I dared not ask? What did I imagine myself becoming? What was most important to me when I was twelve? fifteen? eighteen?

I thought I remembered my adolescence well. I remembered the teachers I liked and learned from, and I remembered the groups of friends I had. But reading books written by other women teachers and researchers such as Maureen Barbieri, Mary Pipher, and Carol Gilligan about the experiences of girls has caused me to look back on my own adolescence with fresh eyes. These authors have documented important data about the nature of growing up female. These data point to aspects of girlhood I had not previously recognized in myself or in the girls I teach.

In *Sounds from the Heart*, Maureen Barbieri (1995) tells stories about girls from her classroom who avoid conflict at all costs, sacrificing their authentic opinions and feelings if these conflict with the opinions of their classmates. These girls are not always conscious of their behavior. Carol Gilligan writes that girls "see a world comprised of relationships rather than of people standing alone. A world that coheres through human connection rather than through a system of rules . . ." (1982, p. 18).

Gilligan and Barbieri's obervations rang true for me. I found myself digging into old boxes and rereading my middle school and high school journals. I saw my own adolescence reflected in what these women write about growing up as a middle-class, Caucasian female, and I began to look at my female students differently.

Carol Gilligan writes, "The knowledge about relationships and the life of relationships that flourish on this remote island of female adolescence are like notes from the underground" (Gilligan, Lyons, and Hamner 1990, p. 24). I kept notes to myself all through middle school and high school. I would often jot down exactly what happened in a day, or how I was feeling about a certain event. I never imagined that I would look back on these writings with adult eyes and see how they reflect a girl's experience and perspective. These notes might look or feel familiar to other women teachers. They may bring back memories for them about what life was like as adolescents.

The following excerpts are taken from my seventh-grade diary. This series of diary entries clearly illustrate Gilligan's observation that girls see a world that coheres through human connection.

March 11, 1982

Sorry I haven't written, but I guess I forgot. How have you been? These days have been going pretty boringly. My mom and dad got back from Hawaii and Jennie went to Tahoe for her 13th birthday. She got back yesterday. I found a ten dollar bill in the laundromat. I didn't tell anyone though. I'm still second chair but tomorrow is the challenge. Tim finally admitted he likes Lisa and Daniel's not a brat anymore. That's the news.

A few days later I wrote:

First of all, Tim and Lisa were going together. Then they broke up then they went together again. Now they're broke up and hate each other. Jennie was secretly in love with Tim but now she hates him too! I don't know what to do!! Tim is my friend, but so is Lisa and Jennie. Right now I'm kind of mad at him but I know it won't be for long.

My own personal opinions are not as important as maintaining group cohesiveness in this situation. I want to maintain my connections with Tim, but my best friends, Lisa and Jennie, don't like him. The last thing I would want to do is create confict in the group, so really, I am in a terrible bind. Luckily, a few days later I wrote, "Jennie and Lisa aren't mad at Tim anymore. So I don't have to worry."

Looking back on this series of observations about friends, I recognize now that I was seeing a world connected through relationships. I could not separate myself from what was going on with the entire group. Mary Pipher, a psychologist who has written extensively on adolescent girls, states that "girls, who tend to do better in relationship-based, cooperative learning situations, get lost academically in [jr. high school] settings" (1994, p. 64). The following is an excerpt from my eighth-grade journal on cooperative learning situations:

In Social Studies we are split into groups and our group was Tim, Daniel, Jennie, Lisa and me, but Tim and Daniel were goofing off too much so we split up into two groups. Tim and Daniel and us three. We were doing just fine until they started acting like they wanted back in our group. We said no. They found out we were copying right out of this work sheet, but they said they wouldn't tell. Then we all got mad at each other, and after school, Tim called Jennie and told her that they had told the teacher and we were going to get into trouble. I think it's a lie to get back at us just to scare us. I don't think they would tell and I don't think they even had time to tell. But Jennie thinks they did. I am supposed to call her tonight to find out if anything more has come of it. Other than that, it's been a pretty ordinary day. (Boring) B-

My attention to group dynamics in eighth grade astonishes me. Sentences like "we all got mad at each other" make me wonder who *really* got mad and who just followed along? I recognize what I think in this situation, but I also pay attention to what others think. My opinion does not rule; it takes a back seat to the opinion of the group.

These same sentiments prevailed in high school. This entry is taken from my journal in an advanced writing class:

My objective for this course is not to become "Advanced," because that would be putting me ahead of other people who write, and I don't believe that my writing or my thoughts are more "advanced." My objectives are to improve my writing through practice, to learn about what others write and how they go about it, to learn how to listen well, and, of course, to discover my own ideas and develop them.

I find it both fascinating and telling that "discovering my own ideas" is last on my list. Listening well and learning from others come before actually discovering my own thoughts. These discoveries about who I was and my emphasis on the needs of the group over my individual thoughts and ideas are important because they are still a part of who I am today. And, it is important to recognize this attribute in the girls I teach, especially when the messages girls are receiving lead them to sacrifice their sense of self in order to fit in. Mary Pipher writes, "Girls have long been trained to be feminine at a considerable cost to their humanity. They have been evaluated on the basis of their appearance, and caught in a myriad of double binds: achieve, but not too much. Be polite, but be yourself" (1994, p. 44).

Adolescence is a time of intense emotional turmoil. Self-doubt and dramatic emotional ups and downs are somewhat normal for both sexes. Unfortunately many girls, myself included, have a difficult time pulling through the storm of adolescence with our sense of self intact.

My own decline in self-esteem is documented in my journals. I first began to experiment with makeup in the eighth grade. I also started to be self-conscious of my physical appearance at that time. The following are pictures I drew of myself after wearing makeup to school for the first time. The first picture shows me without makeup; the second is a drawing of me with makeup. I wrote, "Today I wore makeup to school, and all anyone said about it was that it smeared. I'll never wear makeup again" (see Figure 2.1). Then I drew a picture of myself with makeup on (see Figure 2.2).

I found equally telling journal entries in one of my high school notebooks. For me, like many young women, being popular became a number one priority, and physical appearance had a lot to do with it (see Figure 2.3). The list in Figure 2.3 tells a story, not just about me, but about the struggles of many girls, then and today. Being skinny in high school was first on my list. Smart comes sixth, and talent ranks a low eighth. One of the positive things I say about myself is that I'm "not ugly." On the negative side, I say I am "shy" and "unwilled." It is as though I recognize the predicament I am in but believe that by being physically beautiful I will gain a sense of self and become confident and determined. Seeing myself as a part of a larger group, I want "to fit in," "to be loved," and "to say the right things."

Another chart, created the same year, is also telling (see Figure 2.4). I'm not sure what B.F. stands for on this chart, but Diet comes first, then Friends and Family, Face, Clothes, Mood (does that mean to always be in a good mood?) then Homework and Grades. My list

Figure 2.1 The author's adolescent self-portrait without makeup.

of exclamations at the bottom of the chart is, I believe, my own recognition that somehow this chart represents a not-so-healthy set of values, but I didn't have any other way to rearrange them in my life. I spent a great deal of my time in high school focusing on my weight. Thus, I spent a great deal of time thinking about food. Figure 2.5 shows an excerpt from a diary on food. I have many entries like this, listing what I have eaten for the day.

Figure 2.2 The author's adolescent self-portrait with makeup.

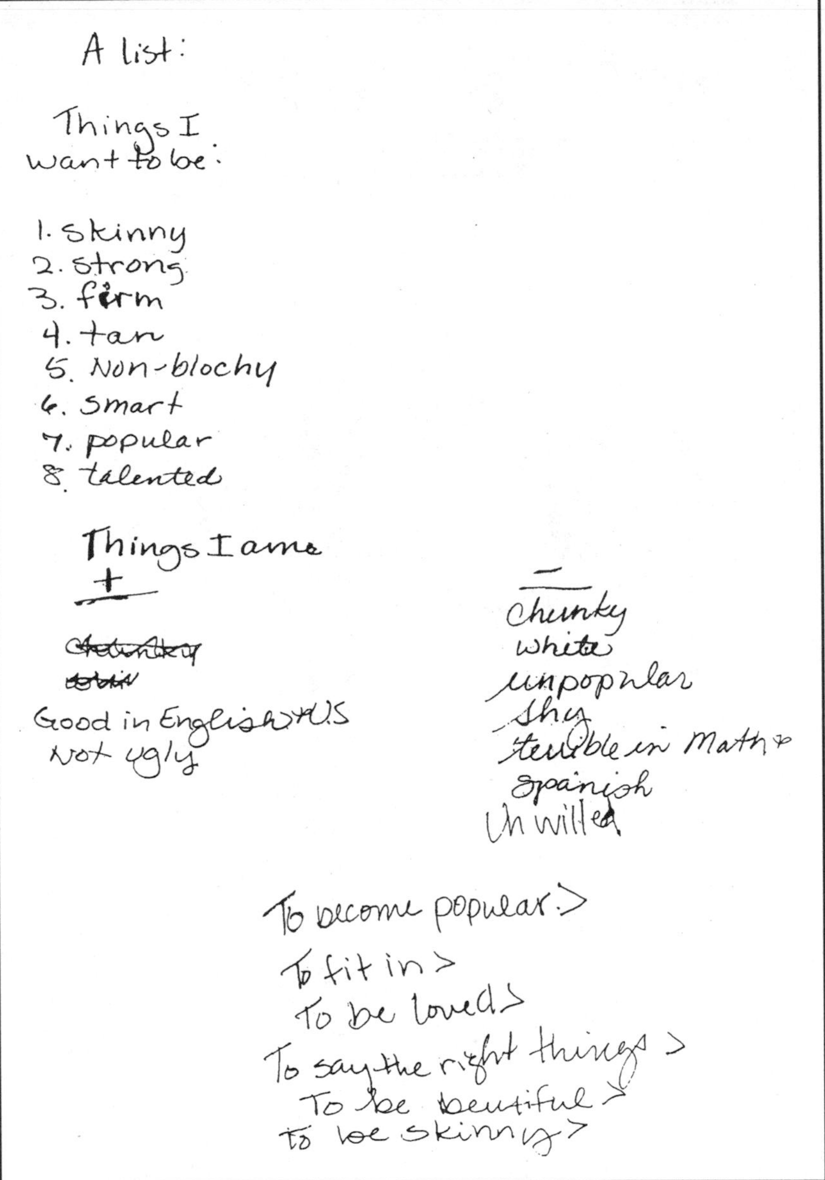

A list:

Things I want to be:

1. skinny
2. strong
3. firm
4. tan
5. Non-blochy
6. smart
7. popular
8. talented

Things I am

\+

Good in English + U.S
Not ugly

\-

chunky
white
unpopular
shy
terrible in Math + Spanish
Un willed

To become popular >
To fit in >
To be loved >
To say the right things >
To be beutiful >
To be skinny >

Figure 2.3 The author's adolescent "List of Priorities."

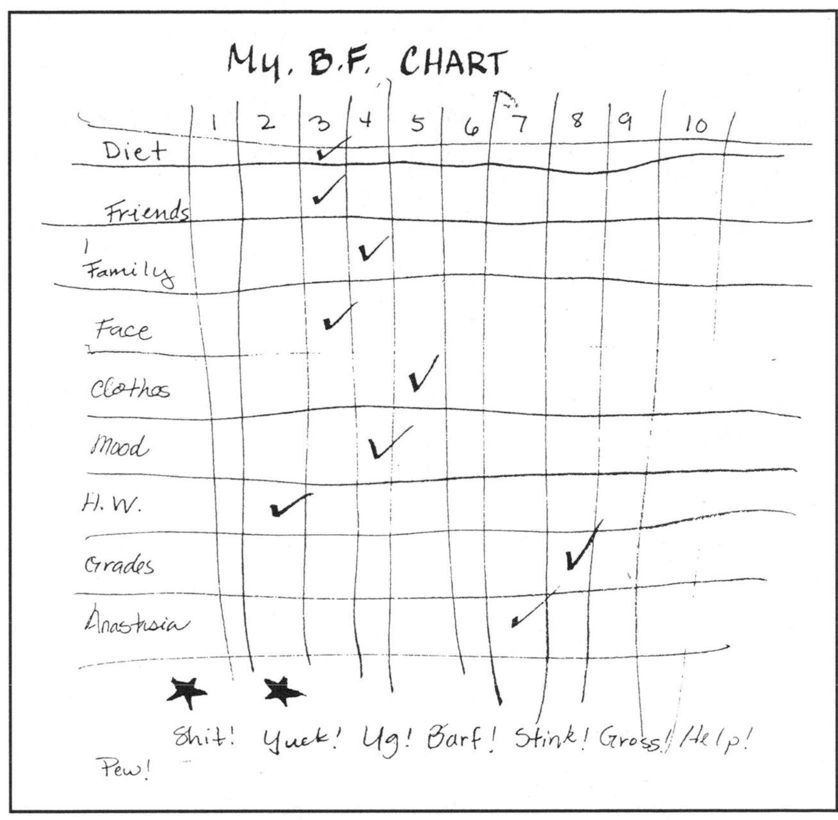

Figure 2.4 The author's adolescent self-ranking chart.

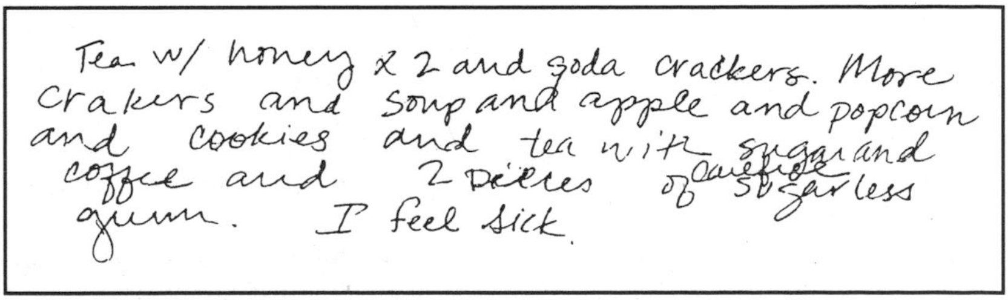

Tea w/ honey x 2 and soda crackers. More crakers and soup and apple and popcorn and cookies and tea with sugar and coffee and 2 pieces of Carefree sugarless gum. I feel sick.

Figure 2.5 "Food" excerpt from the author's adolescent diary.

The following quote is something my best friend Rachael said to me when we were seniors in high school:

There's something seriously wrong with me. I keep eating and I'm getting really big . . . no, it's not just "I'm getting fat" I seriously can't fit into my clothes anymore and I keep going around telling people I'm okay when I'm really not but I just don't want anyone to think that I still have a problem. I can't believe I'm telling you this, I haven't even told my parents.

Rachael was hospitalized for anorexia early on in high school, and by her senior year she was bulimic. Her voice speaks for many high school girls in the '90s as well.

How does all this self-reflection carry over into my teaching? I am keenly aware of the need for most young girls to "fit in," and how difficult it is for some girls to speak to what they really believe. I strive to create situations in which the girls I teach feel safe to express themselves. I want to read between the lines of their writings as I have just done with my own to understand what they are really trying to say. I want to point out to them the dangers of placing so much importance on fitting in. I want to give them opportunities to express their frustrations about growing up female, and also give them strategies to cope. Nicole, an insightful seventh grader, wrote "Girls don't usually get as noticed as much." My intention is to *notice* the girls I teach, not for what our society expects them to be but for who they are and who they are becoming.

References

Barbieri, Maureen. 1995. *Sounds from the Heart: Learning to Listen to Girls*. Portsmouth, NH: Heinemann.

Gilligan, Carol. 1982. *In a Different Voice*. Cambridge, MA: Harvard University Press.

Gilligan, Carol, Nona P. Lyons, and Trudy Hamner, eds. 1990. *Making Connections: The Relational World of Adolescent Girls at Emma Willard School*. Cambridge, MA: Harvard University Press.

Pipher, Mary. 1994. *Reviving Ophelia: Saving the Selves of Adolescent Girls*. New York: Putnam.

A Woman's Silent Journey

Erika Miller

Am I fat? Look at my thighs. Oh God, they're huge, and my hips. Who's going to like me with this body? "Someday my prince will come," Cinderella hums in my ear. No prince will claim me as his bride. I'm too ugly.

Stepping on that scale in the second grade was the beginning of the end for me. Weighing in at 67 pounds was horrifying. As Tinkerbell looked into a hand mirror and realized her hips were too big in Peter Pan, I realized I was fat, enormous, and disgusting. At least that was the image Tinkerbell helped me paint for myself.

Four years later, I actually was overweight, and without an ounce of self-esteem. I was *Seventeen* magazine's nightmare and Disney's newest side-kick. Finally, after years of waiting, my belief that I was fat was validated by jokes and bullying by peers. I silently dreamed about being the skinny, blonde girl in cartoons or the curvaceous model gracing magazine covers.

A year later I was average in size, but I still held the self-conscious behaviors that were initiated in my seventh year. At this time I began my dieting lifestyle. The desire to be thin overtook my body. I kept my stomach in posture at all times, while I powdered my nose and applied lipstick. Instead of concentrating on having fun, my middle school and high school years were spent trying to achieve a perfect face and body.

The summer before my senior year. I discovered a diet that worked. It is called decreasing your food intake to what you need to survive and nothing more. In three months I went from 130 pounds to 103 pounds. People began commenting on how skinny I looked, and that I resembled a walking skeleton. The problem was, that I still looked 130 pounds to myself.

Soon I couldn't control my weight loss. I would wake up in the morning and weigh two pounds less than I had the day before. My hair became dry, my hands cracked and bled, and I lost my period for four months. I came to realize that something was wrong and began forcing myself to eat nourishing food.

I am recovering now, but why is this behavior normal in our society? Why are millions of women starving themselves to death? Has society made being thin this important? So important that women will die for the skinniest body? Why can't we be content with how we look?

The U.S. has an 80-billion-dollar diet industry. Companies are profiting off of our feelings of inadequacy. From birth, Disney taunts us with fairy-tale princesses who would die of anorexia if they existed. They win their men by fluttering eyelashes and innocent giggles (e.g., Snow White, Sleeping Beauty, Cinderella). The only prerequisite for princesses is beauty. And thus it is the only prerequisite for happiness.

By age eight, Mattel's Barbie takes over where Disney left off. This 42–24–32 woman would fall over if she was an actual person. but girls worship her body and dream about looking like her all the same. How can we let this happen? Eighty percent of all fourth-grade girls are on diets, according to a current poll. Why are ten-year-olds thinking about their weight, much less concerned about it? Could Barbie have something to do with this?

When Barbie gets old, *Teen* magazine places itself in adolescent girls' hands. Tall, thin women cover the pages and tempt girls with products to soothe their every need. What? Jimmy doesn't like you? Well, maybe it's because of that zit or those ten extra pounds, or your dull hair. The list goes on and on. We, as women, are never good enough. Not good enough for men and not good enough for each other. We compare ourselves inwardly, while swearing our hips and thighs are the biggest to have ever walked the earth.

We need to change the way people think about women. We don't need to be sex objects who live to please men. Times have changed and are continually changing. We must no longer be dominated by male fantasies of what a woman should be, because we are all intelligent, wonderful people who have a lot more to offer than a slim body and a pretty face.

3

"What Does *She* Like?": Choosing a Curriculum for Girls

Sharon Frye

MONDAY MORNING hall duty. The hallway is bustling with middle schoolers jostling their way through the crowds. Most pay little attention to me, though I nod, smile, and greet them. A moment later a group of girls emerge. They are bursting with energy, popping and bubbling as they approach me.

"Ms. Frye!" The voices overlap each other, bright with excitement.

"Ms. Frye, what are we doing in Art and Literature Workshop today?" The girls swarm around me anxious to know what I have planned for them, talking all at once and leaving no time for me to respond to any of them. "Do we get to read some more poems?" "What kind of story will we read today? I really liked 'Eleven.' " "Are you going to have us do another art project?" "I like how we always sit in a circle." Their enthusiasm is contagious. I'm thrilled they are so engaged in this class. I look from one to another and try to give them a sneak preview of today's class. Before long, it is time to shoo them off to their next classes. They walk away, still chattering about Art and Literature Workshop.

Art and Literature Workshop is the ten-day exploration class I created as part of a multidisciplinary program in our school that integrates curriculum based on semester-long themes. The program is multiage, so students remain in the same classroom with the same teacher for each of their sixth-, seventh- and eighth-grade years. We decided to offer rotation classes, allowing students to choose a focus they wanted to explore in connection with this semester's theme, Expression. These classes met for one hour each day for ten days.

My class was especially created to engage middle school girls. I had noticed that several of them remained quiet in our regular class in spite of encouragement and a focus on developing an emotionally safe learning environment. I also worried that too much of the material we read either focused on male protagonists or was chosen to get boys excited about reading. The girls read what they were asked to and did the assignments, but they didn't seem to connect with the stories we read in class. I wanted them to find connections, to see themselves in literature. I also wanted boys to learn more about themselves and others. They tended to avoid dealing with feelings or relationships. They needed to be able to empathize and learn to be more compassionate and sensitive. The rich and evocative language of the literature I chose explored what it means to be human, how people feel and interact with each other. I wanted my students to experience these beautiful pieces and discover something about themselves in the process.

Overall, the class seemed to be working for the girls. They were enthusiastic, enjoyed the stories and poems we read, made connections with characters and insightful points during class discussions, created beautiful pieces of artwork, and regularly wanted to stay after class or come back after school to continue working on their projects. In their daily journals and later in reflections, they noted they appreciated being able to feel creative, explore different styles of writing, work on projects that reflected what they were thinking, connect with stories, and "learn about myself and others." I was thrilled and invigorated by their enthusiasm. And although it took a while to see how the boys were benefiting from this approach, by the end of the second week I was convinced I needed to continue this kind of focus.

The boys, on the other hand, were more problematic, and during the first few days of the class I found myself questioning my methods. While the girls seemed engaged, the boys, many of whom were sixth graders, made this class difficult for the girls (and me) to enjoy. I spent more time than I wanted keeping them on task. They joked around, bantered with each other, and complained, "This is stupid!" "Do we *have* to do this?" "She [the protagonist] is nothing but a crybaby."

It was frustrating to realize the girls were receiving less of my attention than the boys. The girls were focused; the boys were not. I almost threw out the stories I had so carefully chosen, stories that had female protagonists and dealt with issues of relationships and feelings. "This just isn't working," I thought. But then I considered the girls and what they were getting out of the class. Their artwork was incredible. After reading "Eleven" by Sandra Cisneros, Julia, an eighth grader, drew a person inside a large tree with black pastel to illustrate how people have many different layers (see Figure 3.1). She told the class she could really relate to the protagonist when she talked about sometimes feeling like she was only three and needed

Figure 3.1 Julia's tree person.

to cry like a three-year-old, even though she was eleven. Elizabeth, a seventh grader, wrote about her connection with the story in her journal,

It [the story] reminds me of when I was in the 4th grade I had done my best on a paper in class, and I was feeling so good when I turned it in, but 10 minutes later the teacher calls up me and the mean boy next to me. She asked us, "Why are both of your answers exactly the same?" I was shocked! The boy next to me had cheated off my paper! But he turns to me and says, "Elizabeth, why did you cheat off me?!?!" I was sooo mad! Even more when the teacher gave me a lecture on cheating! I just wanted to sit down and cry my eyes out.

This journal entry contained much more voice than I had heard from Elizabeth before. She was very quiet in class—a good girl who did her work and stayed out of trouble. I wondered if this incident helped condition her to keep her voice to herself. Anne, a sixth grader wrote,

I made most of a connection through the "Eleven" story. I connected mostly to that one because I'm eleven and I feel all the ages she does in the story, especially age 6, because I'm always hyper, like a little kid is. Another connection I made was when the teacher asked if it was her sweater even though it wasn't, and then the teacher said that she remembered her wearing it even though it wasn't hers and then making her keep it, even though she didn't want to and it wasn't hers. The way I connected to that is because people accuse me of something I didn't do or having something that isn't mine. An example is yesterday when someone was sitting at my desk they left all their stuff on my desk and I gave the stuff to them, but since it was my desk they wanted me to deal with it. I hate it when people do that.

I had never seen this girl act hyper. In class she was reserved, quiet, and competent. These examples illustrated the kind of safe atmosphere I was trying to create—an opportunity for girls to practice sharing their voices. How could I get the boys involved without sacrificing what was good for the girls? I decided to tough it out a little while longer, hoping the boys would come around.

The third day I read an excerpt from Michael Dorris' *A Yellow Raft in Blue Water*. In the section I chose, Christine is telling the story of a dare she took as an adolescent. After I read the piece aloud we had a good discussion about the important role Christine's brother played in her life and how easily she was influenced by peers to do something dangerous. Well, at least the girls had a good discussion. The boys were there and sat in the circle, but they fidgeted, made jokes about the story, or didn't contribute at all. "At least," I thought, "the girls are talking." Next I asked them to divide into groups of three or four to create a group illustration of what they felt was the central point of the story. I purposely let them choose their own groups. I wanted to see if the girls would stick together. They did. The girls' groups got to work right away. They formed circles around their pieces of butcher paper, discussed what they wanted to illustrate and what materials they wanted to use, and divided up roles to complete the project. One group created a beautiful pastel drawing of Christine crossing a natural bridge and her brother holding his arm out to encourage her. Another divided their paper into fourths, creating a comic-book-like frame, so one of their members, who had cerebral palsy, could more easily work on her section. They talked as they created these pieces, sometimes about the story and other times about events in their lives. They were connecting with this book and were proud of their work.

The boys' groups rebelled. They goofed off and joked around. Several of them told me, "There's no point to this dumb story." At the end of the class period both boys' groups scrambled to complete something. One group used a giant fuchsia marker to write the title of the book in large block letters on their paper. The second group colored in a blue blob, which they informed me was the river (under the natural bridge). As they were finishing their masterpieces one of the boys noticed some of the girls' work and commented, "Oh, wow. Their stuff is gooood." I replied that you could really tell they hadn't just thrown something together at the last minute.

That night as I read their journals I noticed that nearly every boy commented on how their groups had not worked very well together, while the girls felt their groups were productive. The girls remarked on their conversations with each other about family, relationships, jealousy, peer pressure, trying to be perfect, and trust. Big issues to talk about. Maura wrote in her journal,

I think the point of it [the story] was jealousy leads you to the worst. It is also about how nobody is perfect. And about how girls can be friends with their brothers and that girls can be better than boys. And how dares can get you into real trouble, but most of all the safety and companionship between every sibling.

I was struck by the number of ways Maura related to the story. It was a rich piece of literature for her. Elizabeth also found ways to make meaning from the story. She wrote,

The author probably wrote this story because it teaches a lesson on not doing anything that is too physically dangerous, and to appreciate the people in your lives and what they do for you.

Although the girls seemed to find their conversations surrounding this story engaging, the boys were unhappy with the quality of their work and recognized they had wasted their time. A couple of them asked for the chance to try the assignment over. In his journal Todd, a sixth grader, complained,

It was hard to work with my group, because they were goofing off. I drew a picture of a cool dude and his sister going to fall off a bridge. There's no point special. I don't know. I think we could do better.

Todd was struggling with this assignment. He knew he was capable of more than he accomplished.

I decided to comply with the boys' request and found their second attempts were somewhat better. The artwork itself was still of questionable quality, but the discussions they engaged in were much more meaningful. They found ways they could relate to Christine. They understood how she could be jealous of her brother and adore him at the same time. And they debated whether or not they would have taken the dare she had. They were starting to make connections.

By the fifth day it was apparent the class was finally working for nearly everyone. We read a poem by N. Scott Momaday titled "Delight Song of Tsoai-talee" from *In the Presence of the Sun*. We picked out our favorite lines, created our own metaphors, and wrote additional lines to add our voices and connect our lives to the poem. Then I asked them to make an artistic representation of their connection with this poem. Both boys and girls eagerly engaged in the project. Nearly everyone was anxious to share their work when they were done. Julia found images in magazines of her connections with the poem and cut them to form a collage of a person (see Figure 3.2). She wrote in her journal, "I am a beam that highlights the stars. I am the sparkling piece of sand among crumbs of rock." Maura, a sixth grader, created a collage with her favorite lines, her own lines, and pictures with connecting images. One of the lines she wrote was "I am a flower being born." Near that line was the picture of a baby in the middle of a yellow tulip. The boys were much more engaged in their artwork. Christopher, a sixth-grade boy, created a poster with a photograph of a moose outlined in black and surrounded by orange and yellow pastels. Below the moose was a modified version of a line from Momaday's poem: "I am a deer standing in the dusk!" (see Figure 3.3). The journal entries also reflect the class's enthusiasm for this project. Maura wrote about her piece, "I love my collage. I cannot believe I found so many good clips! It expresses me wonderfully." Christopher turned his journal entry into a poem.

I am like a poem. I have rhythm and beat, sound and feeling.
I can be alive, alive and roam the earth like a person,
like a child, like a people or animals in the trees.

The final story we read was Charlotte Watson Sherman's "Emerald City: Third and Pike." With this story we talked about our dreams and again, nearly everyone was engaged. The class discussion had a component that was missing from our first few class discussions. Both boys and girls offered opinions, made inferences, and shared their personal dreams.

One of the most important reasons I decided to have my students keep daily journals was to give girls who are uncomfortable with speaking up in class a place to express their thoughts and opinions. In journals they can explore what they think without worrying what their friends will say or think. Journals also allow me to have a private conversation with each of my students. In general the girls responded to the journals with much more enthusiasm than the boys. Girls wrote on average a page a day, while boys wrote a sentence or two. Boys complained, girls asked for more time to write. Girls responded

Figure 3.2 Julia's collage.

Figure 3.3 Christopher's deer.

to my comments from the previous day's entry and boys often ignored them. Interestingly I noticed the girls' journal entries quickly became personal. They used the stories to explore issues in their own lives. Maura made a strong connection with Rachel in "Eleven." She wrote,

Sometimes I hate being 11 and I want to be two or three and that's okay. People accuse me of things that are wrong. I feel sick and sometimes I cry and get embarrassed. I feel like this is a biography. Why do teachers never understand? Life is so unfair. I have had this experience before and [when] I got through I just wanted to hide. My face gets red and teary. I don't understand why parents say, "Why don't you act your age," but I have more than one age. I am 1, 2, 3, 4, 5, 6, 7, 8, 9, 10, and 11 all rolled up in one.

Maura's own feelings were validated through this story, and in her journal entry she was able to explore her reactions to certain events.

For other girls the journal entries quickly became a way for them to connect with me in a personal way, and were a valuable tool for me in getting to know these girls. They wrote about what I asked them to, but also about what was important to them. After the fourth class, Elizabeth's journal entry had little to do with the story we read. The parentheses are hers.

Dear Ms. Frye,

The brother dies in Vietnam?! How sad!! How does she handle it?

This weekend (on Sunday) I'm going to be in a horse show (cool!), and this is going to be my first time jumping in a show. Of course, my mom is nervous, but I understand why. I really hope I do well, but what if I end up like Christopher Reeve?

Elizabeth had a lot on her mind, and her journal was a way she could let me know what was going on and include me in her life.

Journals became a way for girls to connect with each other as well. I was surprised to find out they shared my responses to their journal entries with each other. Following my response to Elizabeth's journal, another girl wrote in her journal a response to what I had written.

Boys are hard to rope in; they put up a fight and cause us to choose material we think will engage them to avoid classroom management difficulties. Girls, on the other hand, will often do what we tell them to do in school. They work at pleasing the teacher and are often quietly on task.

From the beginning of my teaching I noticed how easy it was to focus on the boys. They demanded my attention. After I read Maureen Barbieri's book *Sounds from the Heart* I became more concerned that girls in my classes did not lose their voices. The stories Barbieri shared of her students' experiences are familiar to me. I remember feeling like her girls felt. I remember saying things I didn't really believe to preserve a friendship. I remember being quiet in class, unsure of myself and unwilling to take risks. I don't want girls in my classes to be afraid or unwilling to speak their opinions. In *Sounds from the Heart,* Barbieri quoted one of her students:

If I don't say what I really think, because I'm worried about how my friends will take it, when I just pretend to agree with everyone else and if I do this all the time, if I do it a lot, then pretty soon I forget what I actually think, and then I start to forget who I really am. (1995 p. 117)

Girls need to have the chance to know what they believe.

Choosing stories and methods especially for girls was a risk for me. Girls deserve the opportunity to express and find themselves in the literature we study. But how would the boys react? How would a curriculum designed for girls help them if the boys were so disengaged they disrupted the class beyond productivity? Is it possible that what is good for girls is also good, though difficult, for boys? Based on this class, my answer would have to be yes. Although we had a rocky start the boys ended up benefiting through an increased awareness of emotions and relationships. They were able to empathize and make connections with the literature they read. They even ended up enjoying the class, and several boys wrote in their evaluations that we should offer the course again. Persevering was worth it. The girls benefited tremendously from a class designed to meet their needs. They spoke up frequently, offered their opinions, made connections with the literature we read, and applied these stories to their own lives. They complained loudly when the class came to an end. Becca wrote, "I am just like 'Eleven' and right now I am eight, because I don't want to stop going to rotation class." Maura wrote in her self-evaluation at the end of the class, "I'm usually really shy and I think this class helped me open up more." Elizabeth wrote, "I really enjoyed this class and it showed in my performance, participation, and attitude in class. I liked the activities and things we did. I wrote a lot in my journal every day completely and I liked writing in it. All in all I did a great job." It worked for the girls.

Reference

Barbieri, Maureen. 1995. *Sounds from the Heart: Learning to Listen to Girls*. Portsmouth, NH: Heinemann.

4

Grab onto Anyone: Women Working with Girls

Maureen Barbieri

I

It is a day of celebration. A group of eighth-grade science students, Class 809, has completed research on clouds, and they are now ready to present their projects—replete with writing and art—to each other and to invited members of the school staff. I am impressed and delighted with the detail and thoroughness in their work, as I discover more about clouds than I have ever known before. I move around the room reading journal after journal, amazed that these students, almost all recent arrivals from China, have accomplished so much so fast. "Make sure you look at Casey's," Kiran Purohit, their teacher, tells me.

As I approach Casey, she averts her eyes. "It's not good," she says. "I have problems." I reach for her journal and begin to turn the pages and read her words. Suddenly I feel her two hands grip my arm. "Can you help me?" she asks. "Can you please help me?" Now her eyes are on mine, boring in, urgent.

"What do you need?" I ask, surprised. "How can I help?"

"I need more English," she answers. "I need a chance. We never get a chance. At home we don't speak English, and in school there is almost no way, no chance. Everyone always speaking Chinese all the time. My writing—I know more ideas than I can say in English. I know I need more English."

I read another page of her journal and tell her how impressed I am that she has included such detailed information. It is clear that she understands how clouds form. But Casey is not pleased. She scrunches up her face and repeats, "I need more English. My English is no good. I know it."

To me the problems with syntax are minuscule when compared with the substantial content knowledge she has articulated with freshness and grace. I want her to feel proud, but she refuses to accept the smallest compliment on her work, chagrined because she knows her grammar and spelling are not perfect.

"My mother told me to grab onto anyone," she insists. "Anyone who can help me learn more English. Can you help me?"

I am struck by the passion in her voice and ponder her dilemma. I am not her teacher, but I am an English-speaking adult who works in her school. As a staff developer, I am in classrooms most of the time. Casey is offering me a real challenge. How might I help her?

Several days later, three girls from another eighth-grade class approach me. "Can you get us into another class?" they ask. "We are not getting enough chances to read. We don't get enough practice in English." These girls are part of a transitional ESL class, Class 816, composed of fairly newly arrived Chinese students receiving instruction in English. Clearly, they believe they should be doing more. Again, because I am an adult working in their school, they assume that I have some say in where they are placed. Again, I wonder how I might help them.

Their middle school—grades 6, 7, and 8—is in Chinatown, New York City, and consists of 1400 students, 85 percent of whom are Chinese immigrants, approximately 700 in ESL-bilingual programs. The girls are right to be worried. They are right when they say this school doesn't give them enough opportunities to speak English. And they are right when they say they are not learning enough.

This is true for a variety of reasons, but one of the most significant is that their classes are simply too big. No matter how talented and devoted their teachers may be, there just isn't enough time in a forty-minute period to ensure that each voice will speak and be heard. The sad fact is that many students, usually the more compliant, docile girls, suffer from neglect. They slip between the cracks because nobody has the time or the energy to allow, invite, encourage, and yes, to *require* them to speak. And Casey and the girls from 816 know it. Fortunately, there is something in them that knows things can be different. They are resisting the status quo, resisting the quagmire of low expectations, resisting apathy.

Classrooms are overcrowded throughout the country, but especially in our inner cities, making it next to impossible for teachers to develop the close relationships with students, particularly female students, that researchers like Carol Gilligan claim are crucial to their development. The union contract limits middle school classes to 32 students, but some are even larger. Teachers struggle to present coherent lessons, set up groups, and facilitate class discussions. Concern for gender issues all but vanishes in most classrooms where maintaining order is almost always the first priority. Quiet, complacent, acquiescent girls are ignored, or perhaps appreciated, but rarely challenged to speak out (Sadker and Sadker 1994).

Knowing this makes the girls' requests all the more poignant and all the more compelling to me. Of course, I have no recourse when it comes to their schedules; I cannot switch them to other classes. What I can do, however, is to think about ways to help them after school, to supplement what they are getting during the school day with something more. When Danling Fu, professor at the University of Florida and monthly consultant at our school, comes to work with teachers, she and I meet to talk to the girls about their lives, about what they think they need from school. They lament the fact that they are not challenged. "We don't do much here; we read baby books," they tell us. "If we try to speak English in the halls or in the cafeteria, people laugh and say we are show-offs."

Friday's Feisty Females

KIRAN AND I decide to form a small group to meet on Friday afternoons. We have been moved by what we have read about women working with adolescent girls and believe Carol Gilligan's theory that such work can be "transformative" (Gilligan 1993, p. 166). Inspired by Karen Karp, we call our new group Friday's Feisty Females. Our idea is to offer the girls opportunities to read and discuss books, to keep writers' notebooks where we will all record our observations, impressions, and questions about our lives, and to make visits to museums and other parts of the city, talking at length about our reactions. Excited and eager to get going, Kiran writes invitations to twelve eighth-grade girls, including the ones who approached me about helping them. Kiran chooses girls she believes will want to participate in something "extra" and who will be diverse, including girls already fluent in English. The girls seem intrigued with the idea.

In preparation for our first meeting, we purchase copies of Carolyn Coman's *What Jamie Saw* and spiral notebooks. Twelve girls show up that first Friday ready to go. Instead of passing out the books or asking them to write, we urge the girls to tell us what they would like the group to be. What are their ideas for spending this time together? "No reading," Jasmine says. "We get enough reading in school." I look at Kiran; her face is a reflection of my own disappointment. This is not what we have envisioned. Jessica agrees. "Let's do something fun."

Jasmine wants to see movies, and another girl mentions a Broadway play. What about a museum? I offer. Silence. Kiran and I exchange glances and silently agree that writers' notebooks will go on hold. Kiran talks about how much she loved *What Jamie Saw*. The girls listen politely—Jasmine looks bored—but don't grab the books.

Finally, Elizabeth asks, "Do you mean that you can just read a book at home when you are sitting around not doing anything? You can just read a book any time, like on the subway or whatever?"

Kiran and I are flabbergasted! "Yes," we say. "Of course you can." I tell them how I read constantly, on the bus, on the train, in the early mornings before getting dressed, late at night after all my work is finished, and Kiran chimes in that her life is also filled with books. Elizabeth is impressed and asks for *What Jamie Saw*.

The most important work we do that day is to establish what "feisty" really means. It is Sarah who raises the question, "What exactly is 'feisty'?" We grab an old dictionary and read, "lively, energetic, exuberant, quarrelsome, aggressive, belligerent." But then we talk. Is feisty good or bad? Is it hard to be feisty? Do they want to be feisty? I tell the girls that I have been moved by their requests, believing that being able to say what you need is indeed a feisty move. We talk for about twenty minutes, although most of the girls are very quiet.

Kiran and I leave the meeting a bit crestfallen. Where is the fire in the belly the 816 girls had shown earlier? Why hadn't they spoken up more? Why had they balked at reading? Could we figure out how to get more girls to talk?

That was our first Friday. During the next week, Elizabeth returns *What Jamie Saw* to Kiran, exclaiming that she has "loved this book" and asking for another. Kiran gives her Patricia MacLachlan's *Baby* and asks Elizabeth to come back with her reaction. Literacy talk in the early morning hours before school starts. Two other girls, Sarah and Jessica, also read Coman's book and agree that it is worthwhile.

Sarah pops into the room one day as Kiran and I are having a planning session. "That book," she begins, "I don't know. That mother is just so, well, she's a disgrace. She has no self-respect. She is lazy." I am stunned. I had expected outrage over the child abuse in the book, but Sarah reacts right away to the female character's choices. "She just sits there smoking and playing cards. She should do something more with her life." I ask Sarah to meet me during lunch so that I can interview her using a tape recorder. "Sure," she says.

What Girls Need Most: "We Want to Be Known"

"Do you think she knows she has choices?" I ask, as we gobble sandwiches.

"She should know. She should just do something."

Whew! I am amazed. Sarah, new to this country, is already trying on adult roles in her reading. "She goes to Earl, and that's the good part," she continues. "He would make a good father. He cares about people; he lets them stay in that—what's it called? Oh, trailer. She could marry him."

"Do you think she should? Do you think she loves him?" I ask.

"Well, no, because when you don't want to do something, and you're forced to, then you're not going to be happy. That's no good."

"Right," I say.

"But if you want your children to be happy—well, she should see how she feels. Earl and the mother are a best-friend type. And when best friends get married, it's kind of mixed up. Friendship and love is not the same. It can't be like a marriage."

"Can friendship be a part of love?" I wonder.

"Yeah, it's a kind of love," Sarah says. "But it's not the same as love-love. It's different. Friends are caring, trying to help people, and love cares too and it does improve. Ah, hoping. But love is kind of like being with each other and helping each other and living together is the good part. Different from friends."

We continue to discuss Jamie and his mother's relationships with Van and with Earl. I am impressed at Sarah's understanding of the complexities of the story and with her sensitivity. Again and again she insists, "This mother should do something for herself and for her children."

I ask her why the girls in our group seemed uninterested in reading at first but then went to Kiran one by one to borrow the book. "When one person says no," Sarah says, "if we say yes, it's like not agreeing with a friend. We don't like to do that."

She thinks for a minute, head tilted a bit to the right. "But Feisties aren't supposed to be like that. They should say what they want." She hesitates and smiles. "But Feisties can still be shy."

I remember the seventh-grade girls at Laurel School in Ohio telling me the same thing (Barbieri 1995). It is next to impossible to find the courage to disagree with a friend; it puts the relationship at risk at a time when the relationship is of vital significance. I know that Sarah has spoken to Kiran about how she is changing, so I ask her to tell me about that. Carol Gilligan's research shows that such conversations are valuable: "When women approach girls as authorities on their own experience and listen to them intently and with respect, girls can speak openly about their thoughts and feelings . . ." (Taylor, Gilligan, and Sullivan 1995, p. 128). I listen intently now to Sarah.

"Are you different this year?" I ask her.

"Yeah, it's like all my friends are changing. Well, let's talk about me first. I am trying to do my work and finish everything by the time I need it. It's like I finish as fast as I could. But the people in my group are trying to do it at the last day, at the end; it's okay, they think. But the teachers describe us by what we do, so we think differently. So it's not my feeling to be with them. We are so different from each other, how can we stay together in friendship?"

"Are you finding new friends?"

"No, not really," she admits.

"That must be hard," I acknowledge.

"Nobody wants to speak English," she says.

"Why do you think that is?" I ask. "Do you get enough chances to speak English?"

"Well, no," Sarah replies. "No, because people in our class, they don't like to speak English. So my friends don't like to speak English because they think that our language is us, so we speak Chinese whenever we want. They don't want to speak English."

"What do you think about that?"

"Well, I think that speaking English is good for us because we are living in America. We have to speak English to live in the world and ask people questions about things. We have to speak English. And my friends say that it is a show-off. They say, 'She always speak English, she always show off like she's white.' But I'm not trying to show off. I am just trying to learn like an American. But I can't because I am a Chinese person."

Gilligan and her colleagues describe "one of the most important benefits of speaking with and listening to girls in this way: it can help girls to develop, to hold on to, or to recover knowledge about themselves, their feelings, and their desires. Taking girls seriously encourages them to take their own thoughts, feelings, and experience seriously, to maintain this knowledge, and even to uncover knowledge that has become lost to them" (p. 128).

I admire Sarah's courage. She knows what she wants and what she needs, and she recognizes that pursuing it will exact a price from her. I see her as a resister, refusing to acquiesce to the pressures of her contemporaries or to what many perceive as her "culture." I feel privileged to have found such a friend.

When Danling Fu comes to our school to help us find ways to move children into English faster, she suggests that teachers encourage more speaking in class. Even though Danling is Chinese herself, several teachers tell her, "But it's in their culture to be quiet. The girls are encouraged to be quiet in this culture. They are more comfortable. We can't go against their culture." Danling reminds us that these girls are here in America now, part of our culture, and must be encouraged to speak. "Where is the beauty in honoring a feudal culture?" Danling asks. And then with quiet eloquence, she insists, "We are just like you. We want to be known."

I think back to my work with American girls in Ohio and recognize the same issues facing these girls in Chinatown. They worry about building and maintaining friendships; they worry about disagreeing in public with teachers or with other students; they wonder whether they will have choices in their adult lives. Culture, to a large extent, defines gender roles. As adult women, it seems to me, we have a responsibility to help our adolescent female students examine what this means to them. In Chinatown, girls must be very assertive if they are to learn English and have real options in higher education and in life. Real literacy is essential, of course, but so is individual attention, the chance to question, to wonder, to lament, to imagine, to speculate, to plan, to wish, to dream big in the company of adult women.

Our First Feisty Trip

KIRAN AND I are eager to have this group jell. We want the girls to read and write, but we don't want to insist. We continue to nudge them by talking about books we think they would like and making sure to have plenty available in Kiran's room. Several begin to read and to tell us, in informal ways, that they are enjoying the books. But we want to do more. We want to help the girls experience their new city, their new culture, by venturing out of school. We want to explore what it means to be New Yorkers, and we know that such exploration will become the heart of our work with the girls. The holidays are approaching, and we decide to take them uptown to see Rockefeller Center. Most of them have not been out of Chinatown, so the subway trek alone will be an adventure. They have balked at the idea of museums, the same way they had initially balked at the idea of reading, so we make a plan to win them over. We are sure that, if we can just get them inside a good museum, their attitudes will change, so we put the Neapolitan Tree at the Metropolitan Museum of Art on our agenda.

Sure enough, the girls are fascinated by the museum itself and pause to marvel at every drawing, every tiny clay pot, every wall exhibit in the hallway. Finally we get to the tree. Sarah stops dead in her tracks and gasps. "What do you think?" I ask her. "I cannot speak," she says. She stares for several seconds and then walks around the tree, studying each carved figure.

The other girls are equally amazed. Abby, mesmerized by the Italian crèche, comes over to me, grips my arm, and asks, "Maureen, is God true?" I am stunned. This is perhaps the most profound question any student has ever asked me, and I feel my throat close. I put my arm around her and say, "Oh, yes, Abby, yes." Kiran, remembering that these girls are probably not Christian, explains, "People believe different things about God, Abby."

Sarah tells us how she sees it: "The lights on the tree symbolize peace and hope. They are shining down on the people who are not so happy. The child in the manger is called the Prince of Peace." She reads the museum description of the exhibit and copies it all down in her notebook, even though we have not asked anyone to do this.

That weekend Sarah writes, unbidden, a piece she calls "Our Feisty Trip," which she presents to me in school the next week. She details every single thing she experienced, including the smell of the Christmas trees on sale on Lexington Avenue, the bus fumes along Fifth, the music in the subway station. But it is the tree that she knows she will always remember.

That tree was not actually a Christmas tree. It was an Angel Tree. When I first looked at it, I got a powerful feeling inside me is going burst out into the open. I told Maureen that the tree is full of hope and dreams. At the bottom of the tree, there is a father, a mother, and a baby son. They all have a ring around their head. The baby is Jesus. He was just born and everybody is coming to see him, the Prince of Peace. There were two sides, one side is full of gods and angels, and the other side is like for humans, normal people and animals. But that day looks like the doors of heaven and earth is open to each other. All those angels on the tree, I think it represents they are giving peace, light, energy, happiness to the world of both heaven and earth. The little candles are for lighting the earth to peace and love. The star on the top is where the angels come from. It is like making the earth from darkness to light and happiness. I love this Angel Tree. It's full of love and peace. It's wonderful to be with it. . . .

Opening the Floodgates: Girls' Need to Talk

WEEK AFTER week, Kiran and I are struck by how much the girls talk. It is as if they have been suffocating in their silence and are now finally gulping for air, grabbing this chance to speak and be heard. I suspect they have been longing for an adult's listening ear, an opportunity to voice their questions, fears, and confusion as well as their impressions, convictions, and memories. Whenever we leave the building, Sarah attaches herself to me and talks nonstop about her life in China—once her cousin was hit by a car, and she still feels responsible—about her schoolwork, about plots of movies she has seen. She says, "People have to dress a certain way to be cool. They want other people to like how they look. They want to be popular. I don't think I am cool. I am not sure." It is a familiar concern.

The girls also worry about where they will go to high school. In New York most eighth graders apply to specialty schools all over the city. If they are not accepted, they must attend neighborhood schools, which in Chinatown are quite large. May, Daisy, and Kimberly hope to go to Baruch College Campus High School, a new small school where they believe they would get individual attention. Sarah would like to go to a school that specializes in art. When I offer to write letters of recommendation for them, most are pleased, but not Sarah. "I want to get into a school because of who I am," she says, "not because of what someone says about me."

The need to be autonomous, individual, and unique, the need to be seen and heard, and appreciated, is strong in Sarah. I explain that the admissions process involves thousands of applications, papers covered with numbers. How will the admissions people even know who she is, if all they have to go on is numbers? She reluctantly agrees to let me help her.

"Do you think my English is strange?" she asks me as we walk. "Do you think I am hard to understand?" I assure her that her English is good, that there is no way I could be as fluent in another language as she is in English, but she remains skeptical. "I don't have a good vocabulary," she insists. "I don't always know the English word for what I mean."

Casey worries too. "I am a lonely person," she says. "In China I had a lot of friends, but here it is different. I don't know why, but it is different." I ask her about her weekends, whether she ever calls anyone on the phone, but she shakes her head no. Kiran and I have noticed her isolation and have attributed it to the fact that she is very new to the school and to the city. But while the other newly arrived girls seem to form themselves into small groups more easily, Casey is always on the fringe of things. Ironically, since it was her plea that helped initiate Feisty Females, she misses more meetings than she attends, claiming to have forgotten the plans again and again. We are frustrated, and we talk to her about this. She is sorry, she says. She will come this week, she promises.

"It seems that everything I touch, I break," she tells me. At the Met, in the gift shop, sure enough, she picks up a silver glass ornament, and it shatters in her hand. She is mortified to the point of tears. "It will take all my treasure to pay for this," she moans. Luckily, the salesperson assures her this won't be necessary; accidents happen. "I don't know why I am so clumsy," Casey laments.

One afternoon, as dusk approaches, we look at the sky, and I remark on how lovely it is, all purple with streaks of white. "Isn't it something?" I ask her. "Oh," Casey replies, "I am not good at art. I'm terrible. Everyone always finished before I do, and mine is always ugly. In ceramics, I break the pots." I want her to enjoy the beauty of the moment, but even now she is hard on herself. Self-esteem is a huge issue for these girls, and we are all too aware of what a challenge we face in helping them see themselves more positively.

We decide to look at more art, with the hope that it will spur conversation about women's roles, women's choices. We arrange to work with a museum educator at the Frick Collection. We will look at several portraits of women and ask the girls to infer or to imagine who they might be, what their lives might be like. The Frick is ideal for our purposes, as it is not as huge or overwhelming as the Met.

On our first visit, we consider George Romney's "Henrietta, Countess of Warwick, and Her Children," although we do not read the work's title at first. "What do you see when you look at this painting?" asks Ashley, our host. "Who do you think she is?"

May, Abby, and Kimberly speak at once, "A mother." Kimberly adds, "She is very kind."

But Sarah has other ideas. "She is not a mother. Or, she is not a good mother. Her heart is not with her children. She is not looking at them; she is looking at us."

Back and forth they go. Kimberly notices that she is holding the daughter in her arms. Sarah comes back to the woman's eyes. I am impressed at their willingness to jump in and speculate this way, to put themselves right into the world of the painting. Sarah whispers to me, "Why do I always have the opinion that nobody else has?" I tell her this is okay, this is great, this is what looking at art is all about. We can't know the truth of these women's lives, but we can try to imagine. The more opinions we have, I tell her, the more possibilities we will be able to consider.

We look at Thomas Gainsborough's portrait, "Mrs. Elliott," and May says, "She is trying to look young. She is wearing too many makeups on her face. She is all painted." The other girls agree. Sarah adds, "She is a bad dresser." No one says, "I don't know" or refuses to answer Ashley's gentle questions. When we come to Jean-August-Dominque Ingres' "Comtesse D'Haussonville," Abby says, "She wants the artist to think she is pretty." Sarah says, "She is just a show-off." They ask Ashley how long these women might have had to pose for the paintings. They wonder about the relationships that developed with the artists. They wonder how the women wanted to be viewed by people who would see their portraits.

Ashley asks us to choose a painting and do a little writing about what we imagine the woman's life to be. Several girls choose Whistler's "Symphony in Flesh Color and Pink: Portrait of Mrs. Frances Leyland" for its delicate elegance and because, in May's words, "it has a feeling of Japan." Mrs. Leyland is peering off into the distance, looking disturbed. Sarah says, "She is going to be married, but she doesn't love the man. That's why she looks so sad." Daisy writes, "She is very sad. She always stays in the house like in jail." And Kimberly writes, "She is sad. Maybe she don't like her husband, but her mother need her to marry him."

Kiran and I are moved by the girls' empathy and compassion. We make plans to do more writing to explore what they have begun here, to look at the choices women have made in the past and are making today, to examine what choices are available to us and to them. Art seems a way to begin, a way to help them express what it is they believe or question. We can talk about the women in the paintings the same way we talk about women in literature, and we can use writing to help us discover what we really think.

But visiting museums and imagining women's lives by looking at paintings will be just part of our work with these young women. We will also invite women from the community and beyond the community to come to our meetings to tell us about their work, their compromises, the satisfaction and the frustration they have found in their lives. There seems no limit to what we can do together, as long as the conversation remains open, as long as we are willing to listen and learn.

The girls go home to lives different from the ones Kiran and I knew as adolescents, different from the lives the Laurel School girls lead. Sarah's apartment is on the sixteenth floor, and often the elevator is broken, so she has to walk up. May is not allowed out except for school activities. All the girls' mothers work in factories or restaurants, often until after 10 P.M. Many have responsibility for younger siblings. But we do have this in common: We are females who want to matter in the world. We want to be respected as ourselves. We want to make connections to other people. We want to make contributions. We want to try our wings and find out just what we can do.

We Are Like You

GIRLS IN other schools have the same need to talk and be heard as the girls in Chinatown have. Across town in Chelsea I meet with a group of seventh-grade girls each Tuesday for forty minutes after lunch, and we read and write poetry together. These sessions evolve into conversations about whatever is on the girls' minds that week—typically their observations of city life, frustration with hypocrisy, or their apprehensions about the future. Their poems reflect their desire to make strong, genuine connections to other people—and the enormous difficulty they have in doing this. We don't have time to take jaunts to art museums, but we do value the chance to talk. I like to think that there are hundreds of such groups—women meeting with girls—in schools all across our country. I like to think women teachers are making little pockets of time to get to know what is on girls' minds. I like to think girls are finding respite from their crowded classrooms and their crowded lives. In the best groups, of course, women like Kiran are letting girls set the agenda, trusting that listening and responding to girls' needs will be more helpful than preplanning any activity or curriculum. I like to think that girls in these schools all over America are very much like Sarah and Casey and Daisy, calling out, in Danling's words: "We want to be known."

Kiran is a young teacher, in her second year, discovering the unexpected and undeniable joy in working with students, and especially with our small group. And, while I am older, I too continue to marvel at what these girls have to teach me. Their courage and their honesty, their irrepressible need to ask questions, their trust in us, all fuel my determination to make time and places in the school year for real conversations. We will continue with Friday's Feisty Females for the rest of the year and start up again with a new group of Feisties next year. We will read and write and look at art at the Frick and beyond. We will do some fund-raising, so we will be able to go to the theater, to more museums, and to other city sites this year. And we will continue to help these girls talk, talk, talk.

It is our conviction, Kiran's and mine, that these girls can resist all the forces that seek to annihilate their spirits, the cultural traditions, both Chinese and American, that may thwart their becoming fully autonomous and fully connected to other human beings as equal partners, colleagues, and friends. They can develop their values and their viewpoints on all aspects of life—their bodies, family, friendship, careers, politics, education, the arts—and have confidence that these are worthy and valid. They need our help. They could have "grabbed onto anyone," but they grabbed onto us. And every Friday afternoon, we are grateful.

References

Barbieri, Maureen. 1995. *Sounds from the Heart: Learning to Listen to Girls*. Portsmouth, NH: Heinemann.

Coman, Carolyn. 1995. *What Jamie Saw*. New York: Puffin.

Gilligan, Carol. 1993. Joining the Resistance: Psychology, Politics, Girls, and Women. In Lois Weiss and Michelle Fine, eds., *Beyond Silenced Voices: Class, Race, and Gender in United States Schools*. Albany, NY: State University of New York Press.

MacLachlan, Patricia. 1993. *Baby*. New York: Delacourte.

Sadker, David, and Myra Sadker. 1994. *Failing at Fairness: How Our Schools Cheat Girls*. New York: Simon & Schuster.

Taylor, Jill McLean, Carol Gilligan, and Amy Sullivan. 1995. *Between Voice and Silence: Women and Girls, Race and Relationship*. Cambridge, MA: Harvard University Press.

5

"I'm Not Sittin' by No Girl!"

Jill Ostrow

I

"I'M NOT sittin' by no girl!" whined Austin on the first day of school. He was a fourth grader joining our newly formed grades 4–6 multiage class. The majority of this class were students that were in my grades 1–3 multiage classes in previous years. Some of these students had been with me since first grade. But this upper elementary multiage class was a unique experience for all of us—part of a brand new program. How incredibly wonderful it was to have a group of older students, most of whom I knew and had taught in the past!

The majority of these kids knew me well. They knew how the room worked, and were comfortable and familiar with the way it was set up. The new students seemed excited by the classroom environment. They were elated with the couches set prominently in the middle of the room, and with the wooden tables instead of desks.

The kids who had worked with me before took for granted the freedom of movement around the room. There are no seating charts; the kids make their own choices as to where to sit. At times I will put them into groups; at other times they are free to choose their own. They assume that they will have experience working with all the students in our class community because they know that the foundation of our classroom is the idea of community and respect.

On that first day, the kids came in and sat on the couches; that's how we've always begun our school day. There were the usual comments about the uniqueness of our classroom; I was expecting these, but I was not expecting Austin's loud protest. It caught me off guard. Still, I knew I could sit back and let the other kids who have been a part of our community challenge his words.

"Austin, just let her sit there. It doesn't matter—geez!" was Dave's frustrated response to his comment. Kyle rolled his eyes at Austin and shook his head at me and said under his breath, "I can't believe he just said that." Carly, a girl in the class, looked hurt by such a comment, and Tiffany giggled that a girl would want to sit by a boy.

I began to wonder how there could be such a contrast between these students. What would make one boy move away from a girl and another one not even notice? Did it have to do with what went on in their homes, or was it more complicated than that?

This was a pretty homogeneous group. The cultural differences and socioeconomic levels of the families varied only slightly; 98 percent were middle-class white suburban children. Why then were their experiences with gender in the classroom so different? We were considered an "alternative" to the traditional classroom. The sixth graders were not attending the middle school; they were spending the year in a self-contained multiage class. The parents of these students were all fairly progressive educational thinkers who chose to place their children in my class.

When I shared Austin's response with a friend, she said, "Oh, welcome to fourth-grade boys! It's just normal." Normal? Is it normal to be rude and disrespectful to girls just because you're a fourth-grade boy? I have heard comments like this ever since I was in college working toward my teaching degree over sixteen years ago: girls and boys dislike each other when they reach a certain age; they aren't interested in each other. I can accept the fact that boys and girls typically go their separate ways for some years during their development, but should rudeness and disrespect be accepted as normal?

What if Austin had said, "I'm not sitting next to no black kid!"? Would that be acceptable? After all, Austin lives in an all-white neighborhood; he doesn't have any exposure in his immediate outside world with African Americans. Would it be "normal" that because of his age and lack of experience it should be accepted that he be a little racist? No, of course not. Why then is it so readily accepted in classrooms to let negative comments slide by as "normal" when they deal with gender?

"Oh, it's just the age," is a comment I detest. It's an excuse to accept behaviors and attitudes without confronting them. There are physical characteristics that go along with age, and so certain stages of development are anticipated and expected. For instance, this year I made sure I had a package of sanitary pads in a cabinet just in case one of my sixth-grade girls began menstruating. Physical changes occur in girls at or around sixth grade. Having your period isn't an attitude; it isn't a learned behavior. I believe it is wrong to say that when boys are rude, it is normal and healthy and should be expected and left alone.

Children should be given choices. If a boy wants to play with his boy friends, he should be free to do so. But I think there is a danger in allowing boys and girls to get away with statements like, "I'm not letting her play, she's a girl!" I remember watching a playground supervisor accept such a comment from a group of boys playing soccer in the field. Yet when a group of girls were excluding another girl from playing with them, the supervisor told the group they weren't being very nice and should include the lone girl. The very comment "no, she's a girl" was acceptable for excluding a girl from a boys' play group.

I can't speak for Austin's experience in school before fourth grade because that was his first year with me. But I have been in classrooms where comments about gender have been tossed aside as "normal" or acceptable. It was the students who had been with me that spoke in protest to his comment. I don't think this was a coincidence. I believe children's attitudes stem from their history in their school community.

The students who had been a part of our community were accustomed to openness when talking about equality and diversity. Learning about diversity wasn't something we did in November as a theme; it was a constant and continual discussion interwoven with all that we did. When we talk about another culture we don't just learn what foods people eat or what clothes they wear. I try to have the children imagine what it is like to be in a minority group. I ask them to imagine how it feels to be disliked because you have the "wrong" color skin or the "wrong" religion. If kids can begin to imagine what it is like for someone else, it opens the door for empathy and understanding.

Many schools now make multiculturalism a part of their curriculums. Learning about different cultures and diversity is important, but so is learning about racism, religious freedom, and gender inequalities.

A few years ago, my 1–3 multiage class was studying the 1940s and World War II. The kids were learning about the injustices of the war in Europe and how Jews, Gypsies, and other minority groups were being terribly persecuted, especially in Germany. We didn't just discuss why that was wrong, but tried to imagine what life must have been like for those people and talked about other groups of individuals who have been persecuted, in the past and today. After our studies, the students were asked to begin a project in which they were to hide a family in Europe—either Jewish or Gypsy; they decided they also wanted to hide a Japanese American family in this country.

"Jill, our family is going to be called Nomo. They're Japanese Americans and we want to hide them from going to the internment camps. Is that okay?" asked Kyle. I was fascinated by the connection he was making. I stopped the class as they were working in their groups and called them over to the couches.

"Kyle, can you share your family with everyone?" I asked.

"Yeah, sure. We're hiding a Japanese American family instead," he began.

"Were there Japanese Americans in Europe?" interrupted Mark.

"No," Kyle laughed, "But, we want to hide one so they won't have to go to one of the internment camps."

"Did American people hide Japanese Americans?" Chris asked.

"I don't think so, Chris. I've never read anything about it," I answered.

"How come?" And so began a conversation about why certain groups were helped and protected and others weren't. They had associated the persecution of Japanese Americans in this country with the Jews in Europe—a sophisticated link for young children to make. Making connections between minority groups in elementary, middle, and high schools is crucial. And gender connections fit right in.

Emil, who came to our class as a new second grader, had trouble accepting girls as part of his daily school life. After one group experience where he refused to work with Caitlin because she was a girl, I decided to bring up the incident not as a gender issue but as a community problem.

"How did your groups do this morning? Who wants to share first? Caitlin?" I asked.

"Well, we couldn't get anything done because Emil wouldn't help do anything," Caitlin shared.

"Uh-oh, what happens when not everyone in a group helps out?" I asked the class.

"The work won't get done!" chanted the entire class.

"Can anyone explain to Emil why it is important that he help out?" I asked.

"Emil, if you don't help out, the stuff you want to get done won't get done," Ross chimed in.

"Plus," said Megan, "It isn't fair that Caitlin do all the work herself."

"Emil, do you hear what Ross and Megan are telling you?" I asked him.

"Yeah," he said, looking down.

"Can you give Emil some advice as to how he can help out more and can you also give Caitlin some advice as to how she can help Emil so she doesn't get so frustrated?" I asked the class.

"Emil, just do what you need to do. Ask Caitlin questions if you forget. And, Caitlin, if I were you, I'd just do my half and then give the rest to Emil and don't worry about it. Don't do all of it," Kyle offered.

"Emil, do you want to add anything?" I asked him.

"Sorry, Caitlin, I'll work more better, but you need to let me do some of it too," he said to Caitlin.

"You just won't work because I'm a girl and it isn't fair!" Caitlin said angrily.

"Is that true, Emil?" I questioned.

"Man, Emil, that isn't very good for the community. How do you think the world would work if the boys didn't help the girls? It doesn't matter if you work with a girl or not. You just need to work and help," Kyle told him.

"Emil, what is it about working with a girl that makes it hard to work? Is it just hard to work with Caitlin, or all girls?" Megan asked him.

"I don't know," he said.

"Maybe you should think about Megan's question, Emil," I said, and then went on and let someone else share. He did begin to think about his behavior because we challenged it. He saw that the other kids in the class were not only confused but frustrated with his reaction to working with Caitlin. Throughout the year, as he had more experience with working in our community, his negative attitudes about girls began to lessen.

I made a conscious decision to talk about this with the class as opposed to pulling Emil off to the side and discussing it with him. Gender issues are not individual problems; they are cultural issues that affect the classroom community and should be discussed openly in the community.

After the incident this year when Austin commented about sitting next to a girl, I asked the class during our morning meeting, "If an African American child came and sat down next to you right now would you get up and move away?"

"*No!* Man, Jill, that would be sick!" said Dave. Most reactions were similar to his.

"Okay, what about someone who is Jewish?" More nos.

"What about someone who is Chinese? Someone who is blind? Someone who is younger than you?" The kids looked disgusted and confused by my questions. Good. That's what I wanted. "Why then, do you think it's okay to get up and move away from a girl or a boy?" Stunned faces. Silence. They couldn't answer because there was no answer.

"Tell me, what's the difference? Why is it wrong to yell comments about a person's color or religion at them, but it's okay to make nasty comments about a person's gender?" I knew that bluntness was what was needed. Instead of avoiding the issue, I went head on into it and the result was worth it. The new kids began to realize that we were more than just a class of boys and girls; we were a community who, in order to function as one, needed to be respectful of each other.

I have some guiding principles that I bring to the classroom to help my children confront gender issues.

First, I discuss issues openly and treat comments about gender with importance. I don't accept being disrespectful to those of the other gender in our class, no matter what the age of the student. I consider gender issues to be social issues of our classroom community that must be addressed as a whole group.

Second, we discuss issues and comments that come up as a group, and I don't pull children aside. No matter what grade level I teach, open discussion has become imperative for building a respectful community.

Third, I don't call on students, but allow children to share their own work. The emphasis is on the work and on equal sharing of work and responsibility. Research says that teachers call on boys more often than girls during math classes. I don't put myself in the position of needing to choose either a boy or a girl to call on. My room just isn't set up that way. The class is responsible for ensuring everyone has equal time in sharing their ideas together.

It's important that children be responsible for their comments early on in school. The reason why fourth-grader Kyle was so frustrated with Austin's lack of respect for girls is because he has been discussing gender inequalities ever since first grade.

Austin's attitude toward girls changed dramatically over the year. He came to be much more respectful of who a person is, not what a person is. A parent who had helped out in our classroom shared a story with me about how Austin came to the defense of her daughter.

"It was Becca's birthday and Carl, Austin's younger brother, was making a huge scene because he had to share a seat belt with her. She felt horrible. Austin stepped in and told Carl to move over and be quiet. He then told Becca he'd share a seat belt with her. It was so wonderful. What a change."

Austin was still a fourth-grade boy when that incident happened. He hadn't outgrown his old attitude toward girls—he had outlearned it through working in our classroom community. It's not an age thing; it's a respect thing.

Bill of Rights for Girls

Mary Blalock

What's Wrong with Girls?

If you look around at our world, it is not hard to find something that tries to tell you that as a girl, something is wrong with you. Girls are always told there's something wrong with them. TV and magazines seem to say that girls aren't any good unless they're thin and beautiful. It's hard to feel good about ourselves with these demands around us.

Recent studies show how adolescent boys differ from adolescent girls. They found that around the age of eleven (when puberty usually hits) girls begin feeling more insecure. Two thousand six hundred girls were asked how many of them agreed with the statement: "I'm happy with the way I am." In elementary school 60 percent of the girls agreed, but only 29 percent of the high school girls did. While boys are getting more confident, a lot of girls begin feeling bad about themselves and end up making bad choices.

I wish that I had known about this when I was younger, but I had to go through a lot before getting on the right track again. There are a lot of things I wish I could have learned before. So I've created a list of rights girls deserve to help you on your way to womanhood with confidence. There's already been a woman's movement, now it's time for girls to get some respect.

The Right to Like Yourself. If you get into something that interests you, it helps you feel good about yourself. I like to draw and write, so when I'm feeling bad, I go into my room and draw a picture. There are lots of things that you can get involved in that can become a part of you. It will help you create a personality that you can be proud of.

Also think of things that you like and things that gross you out. What foods are yummy? What music is cool to you? What clothes do you like to wear? All this becomes part of you. Don't be ashamed if other people don't like your taste, or it isn't "cool." Like things because you like them, not because everyone else does. A lot of people like things because they have a name brand. All these names say is that it was expensive. There's nothing wrong with buying something just because you like it, not because it will impress other people.

The Right to Like Your Body. This is a big subject with girls. It's almost impossible to avoid all those ads that try to tell us we need to be pencil thin and look like Cindy Crawford if we want to like ourselves. They are totally wrong! A woman's body is supposed to have fat on it so it can make babies, produce the right hormones, and just work right. The models in these ads have little girl bodies, even though they're women. It's rare for females past puberty to look like this, and it's not healthy to try. It's good for you to realize that while these models are supposedly what we want to be, there are all different ways that people can look and they can all be okay. Take a look around you and compare what you see to what the media shows. You'll find that the world has a lot of different ways people can be beautiful.

The Right to Have Your Cake and Eat It Too. Because of the idea that we're supposed to be skinny, there are a lot of girls dieting and getting involved in eating disorders. An eating disorder is when someone starts looking at food not only as just something we need, and something that tastes good, but as something bad. Though dieting is popular, I say "no way!" Food is something we all need so we can live and function like a normal person. When we start dieting, we look at food in a bad way. I know from experience because when I started dieting, I got an eating disorder, lost too much weight, and had to go to the hospital. It wasn't fun and I missed out on a lot of things. When you worry about dieting, you don't have time for fun. Dieting can even cause you to want food more. Many people who try to diet end up getting hungry or craving sweets and eat more than they would have usually. My advice to you is: accept your body the way it is and accept food as necessary. Don't try to diet, no matter what people say.

The Right to Get Angry. I'm not saying that you should yell at people all the time, or get in fights, but there's nothing wrong with just getting mad. Usually when you feel this way, it's for a good reason and it's a signal that something isn't right. I'm sure a lot of people have told you "don't get mad" or "nice girls don't get mad" when you really were angry and you couldn't stop. But it's okay to get mad as long as you use words and express what you feel in a way that won't hurt anyone. It's okay to tell someone you're angry at them and try to work it out. If you just keep it to yourself, nothing will get resolved and you'll end up feeling bad. Don't turn the anger in on your self either, that makes you feel even worse.

The Right to Feel Protected. When we are little, we don't have to look out for ourselves because our parents do the job. But as we grow older we need to protect ourselves from dangerous things. Sometimes things may make you feel scared and weak. If someone is bothering you, it's good to know how to defend yourself. Community centers offer classes in self-defense and martial arts. These classes teach you how to feel strong and fight back if someone is trying to hurt you. Find someone who you can talk to about things that don't seem right and make sure they get worked out. It's hard to feel confident if you don't feel safe.

The Right to Develop Your Brain. Don't be a stupid-head; make sure you keep getting smarter. Sometimes we're afraid people will think we're nerds if we know a lot of stuff. There's nothing wrong with being smart; it makes you a more interesting person. Don't accept things that people tell you—think about *your* opinion about what you hear. Read lots of books instead of watching TV. It's better for your brain and can be a lot cooler than some of the boring shows and commercials. You don't have to be a dweeb, just don't be dull when it comes to your brain. Tests and grades have nothing to do with how smart you are. I'm talking about learning how things work and how life works. You may not be very good in school but that doesn't mean you're not smart in other ways.

The Right to Be Yourself Around Boys. It's fun to flirt and get into relationships, but there's a lot of confusing things that go along with it. Just be sure that you don't get too dependent on boys to tell you that you're a good person. Never change yourself just so a guy will like you. If you change yourself, then they won't be liking the real you, only the show you put on. It's better to wait for a guy who will like you for who you are, than stay with one who doesn't. It's important to feel good about yourself, even if you don't have a boyfriend. Besides, boys aren't the only thing in the world and I'm sure you've heard the expression, "There's other fish in the sea."

The Right to Your Own Role Models. When we grow up, we get all these ideas about what a woman should be like. These aren't always positive ideas, so sometimes we have to find new places to show us what a woman is. Look around for women whom you admire and ask them about their lives: how they became who they are. Take parts that you like about them and use them to create who you want to be. Don't try and be them; be yourself and walk along their path.

6

Breaking Their Silence

Tera Cushman

YOU SAY adolescence is weird. Yep, we know about adolescence; we're *in* it. It's especially fun for girls. Yeah—we know all about the fun little physical changes that usually are at their worst in the middle of math, and we have finally figured out what the phone is for! Yet, there is a difference between our generations. We are finally noticing something that wasn't seen when you were our age: gender problems. How fun! Even though these glitches in the education system have been realized, they haven't been solved. There was a particularly nasty gender imbalance at my school. Last year, when I was in eighth grade, I helped close that gender gap.

My experience is that many girls lose a good deal of their education because . . . well . . . they don't do much in the classroom. Boys are usually the ones who volunteer in class and who participate the most in classroom discussions. Many girls are simply afraid because they have a fear of humiliation. Any kind of humiliation. To be respected and accepted is many girls' main desire. Many girls don't speak out in classroom situations because they fear their ideas will be looked upon as stupid. They fear being laughed at for their ideas. And the boys? They are usually the ones doing the laughing and the shouting, so I don't think they feel the same way.

In my history class last year we had frequent open discussions. The basic idea of an open discussion is that the entire class debates an unsolvable problem without any teacher intervention. It sounds okay, right? Not quite. The discussions usually went berzerk because many of the people in my grade were extremely competitive. The discussions became a kind of competition of intelligence and moral principles. They were sparring grounds for people with vastly different viewpoints. This group of people (almost entirely boys) had one thing: self-confidence. They were sure of themselves and their ideas. Most of the girls, on the other hand, weren't. The girls often found themselves immediately overcome by the waves of opposition they faced.

We had another problem as well. There were only six girls in the grade, compared with twenty-five boys. We felt, to say the absolute least, outnumbered. The girls couldn't effectively count on each other for support in the classroom because there weren't many others to count on. Also, since there were only about three of us in the class at one time, no one really noticed that most of us weren't talking.

Frankly, I didn't notice the imbalance for several years. I was always yelling along with the boys. The first person to notice (thank you, thank you, thank you!) was Miss Plantz, the intern in our class. She took me aside one day and asked me to arrange a meeting with the girls. We met on Wednesday at lunch. She said she noticed that many of the girls (if there can be a "many" out of six) weren't talking at all in the discussions. Suddenly, she was being bombarded by voices. They did feel scared, and at the same time angry and frustrated. They didn't know what to do about it. They were aware of the fact that they were missing out, but they physically weren't able to bring their voices up. The meetings went on, week after week, Wednesdays at lunch. It was sooooooo cool to see the girls who were so silent in class talk so openly about problems. It was obvious that it was helping them to talk about it and to know that there were others like them. However, the meetings always consisted solely of talking, talking, talking, and more talking only about problems—not about solutions. It got old soon, so Miss Plantz helped steer us toward a solution.

Finding the solution to this problem was as annoying as the problem itself. Miss Plantz left and Ellena Weldon, our Spanish teacher, took over as mediator. For a while we lost our goal of a solution and just argued about stuff. Eventually Miss Weldon actually got us to work and after much discussion, we came up with four basic ideas:

- Make the dominant boys change
- Make the quieter girls change
- Let the teachers deal with it
- Have an open discussion about it

The only idea that everyone could agree on (and barely, at that) was the discussion. We decided someone should talk to Mr. Timmons, the teacher in our history class, where most of our discussions took place. I volunteered to do this.

So, I talked about the discussion format with Mr. Timmons. He thought that the boys would react in a negative way to a discussion about a "girl problem." I agreed completely. He also thought we should discuss equal opportunity to speak, as opposed to equal speaking. In a discussion, there are often people who don't talk as much as others because they just don't have as much to say. They will need less time to speak. Everyone may not take up the same amount of time, but everyone should have the same opportunity to say what they want.

We started the first day of discussion. Mr. Timmons began by saying that he noticed an imbalance in the discussions. He wrote two key questions that we were to answer on the board:

What are the problems with the balance in our discussions?

What can you (the class) do to ensure that everyone has an equal opportunity to speak?

Then he turned us loose into discussion, saying he would intervene only if he felt he needed to.

Everyone went completely nuts. Half the class said we should always help the quieter people and center around them. The other half said we should make the quieter people change because it was their problem. Both sides were talking constantly. It was like a session of the English House of Commons. I think I honestly could've thrown a couple of people out the window.

I was so mad, I physically couldn't leave the room. I stayed and talked to Mr. Timmons. He agreed that the discussion was—ahem—not going well. He also agreed that some people might have benefited by a trip out the window. But he also told me to compromise. Some people's viewpoints are ingrained so deeply in them that their view will not change. There is no use in trying to change their viewpoint. But there is use in getting them to compromise. He gave me this analogy: There's a building with facilities only for people who can walk. People in wheelchairs cannot enter or use the building because it is physically impossible for them. There have been numerous requests for the owners to make the building accessible to people in wheelchairs. The owners have three choices:

1. They can tear down the building and rebuild it exclusively for people in wheelchairs.
2. They can insist that since it's a problem only for the people in wheelchairs that they should find their own way to use the building as it is.
3. They can make a few small changes to the original building to make it accessible and usable for people in wheelchairs as well as for people who can walk.

The people in wheelchairs were the quieter people, and the people who could walk the dominant. By making a few changes, the building's owners gave both groups of people equal *opportunity* to use the building. It was not only for wheelchairs, and it was not only for walking. The obvious solution to our problem was to make a few small changes to our original system of conducting discussions. This would create equal opportunity.

It was easy, it was logical, and it was obvious. Yay! The rest of the class thought so too when I gave them the analogy the next day. After another day of discussion, we decided on a set of rules by which discussions would be governed—a kind of constitution. The basic idea of the "constitution" was that the quieter people would have to get a little louder, and the louder people would have to notice the quieter people. In addition, absolutely no put-downs were allowed. Also, no interruptions were allowed. That would save a few hemorrhaged vocal cords.

That's my story. For the rest of the year, we had few problems with discussions. The girls started to talk more, and the boys calmed down. It was pretty cool. The gender gap had significantly narrowed.

Before I end, there are a few more things I'd like to say. First, teacher initiation and assistance is absolutely invaluable when it comes to solving a problem like this one. If not for Miss Plantz, this whole thing would never have started. If not for Miss Weldon, this whole thing would have died. If not for Mr. Timmons, (thank you, thank you, thank you) this thing never would have been resolved. It is often uncomfortable for a student to come forward and talk about a problem. It is essential for a teacher to be aware of how social pressures are affecting the classroom if problems like these are to be solved. If teachers are aware of a problem, then they can take steps to help the students cope with it.

Also, teenagers (it's obvious, isn't it?) like to live by their own rules. I have repeatedly felt and seen this while trying to solve the gender problem. It is obvious that students would react negatively to a teacher ordering them to cooperate. If the students resolve a problem in a discussion, they are far more likely to obey the resolution than if a teacher told them to. The whole class, and I am not an exception, learned much more from having to find the resolution ourselves than we would have if someone told us what to do. Discussion is especially important in resolving gender problems because the resolution will be made especially for that group of people. A resolution won't work unless it exactly fits the group of people it applies to.

I'd also like to acknowledge that girls aren't the only ones affected by gender binding. However, the vast majority are girls. I know, I know: why? I think it is important to know, so I'll tell you my answer. Boys are not as likely to be as quiet as girls for two reasons. First, there is our history. For the majority of our history, boys have been thought (and taught) to be better than girls. This means they are supposed to be stronger, more aggressive, and smarter than we are. This means they are supposed to do most of the talking and participating in the classroom. Their "role" in the classroom is clear: they are supposed to be either funny or smart, but either way they talk a lot. Girls were taught to be quieter and less aggressive, therefore they don't talk as much now. Stereotypes that have been around for ages cannot be killed in two generations.

Also, girls often take opposition personally. In sports, if the coach yells at them to do something, they take it as a personal attack on their entire ability, and their self-esteem takes a nosedive. In the classroom, if people oppose or attack their ideas, they often see it as an attack on their entire personality. Most boys can deal with a coach yelling at them to do something, and are less likely to take classroom opposition to ideas personally. This allows them to put their ideas in the open with more confidence than girls.

Finally, the most important thing in solving gender problems is *getting people to talk*. I cannot stress enough the importance of girls being able to talk openly about their ideas and problems. The meetings we had are going to continue to next year, still dealing with pressures of society on girls. It has helped us gain some confidence and has taught me a whole bunch. Talking about problems lessens them, helps solve them, and it's the only way to stop gender imbalances.

People say that adolescence is a strange time. Yep, we know; we're stuck in it. We are finding out that boys actually can be fascinating people, and that we can talk for hours about meaningless social drivel. However, all too many of us have hit the one problem that most of us would discuss only over our dead body: gender imbalances. But some of us decided to talk about it and fix it. And we did.

7

Putting the Heart in Mathematics: Adding Stories About Girls

Karen Karp

When searching my memory for titles of books that I studied in school, ones that were read with emotion in class, characters that I analyzed to the point of knowing, and plots that I rehearsed over and over, I was stunned. Did so few include important females? When the world is repeatedly described and you are not a part of the picture, the message is not subtle. If girls do not envision themselves as characters who face uncertainty, seek change with a positive attitude, and take risks with confidence, how will they learn to carry out the roles in society we expect them to achieve? How can girls be continuously asked to examine the lives of important men while consistently studying women filling subordinate roles and then think of themselves as problem solvers and leaders?

When girls do not develop mental images of women as capable and logical thinkers but as damsels in distress, is it any wonder that although females are taking more mathematics classes than ever before, they still strategically avoid careers in mathematically related fields? Asking women about their mathematics experiences in schools can generate many stories about ways in which gender influenced their mathematics education. There are tales of the ways they navigated around mathematics courses, responded enthusiastically to a counselor's recommendation to add more English courses to boost their grade point average, or happily accepted parental advice that they would not need calculus. Little did these women know that these strategies would shut them out of many career opportunities and collapse their options in an increasingly mathematical and technological world. Entering the next century innumerate will be as dangerous as it was to enter this century illiterate.

In the critical years between primary grades and high school, girls seem to be put at a math disadvantage. This change of girls' interest and confidence in mathematics during the period between fourth and eighth grade is part of a larger phenomenon. Researchers report that adolescent females often lack a "hardy personality" (Ouellette and Puccetti 1983), a disposition that includes looking forward to changes and challenges, feeling in control of one's life, being responsible for one's own actions, and surviving unfavorable conditions.

These characteristics are also linked to successful problem-solving skills and could be related to the fact that females often lose interest in mathematics at this very same age. When female students lack confidence in their ability to prevail in challenging situations, expecting that they might approach mathematics problems with risk-taking behaviors seems unlikely.

The research in this chapter details ways teachers can help both build "hardy" girls and nurture students to mature mathematically. Three elementary school teachers and a university professor undertook an action research project to probe links between literature and mathematics. Our research is steeped in the research of others who looked long and hard at females' learning styles and the most successful methods for teaching mathematics. Therefore, this chapter meshes the knowledge base of researchers who came before with our experiences in real classrooms.

In our action research project we investigated a strategy for teaching mathematics by providing examples of hardy female personalities through young problem-solving girls and women found in children's literature. These "feisty female" characters acted as springboards to mathematics lessons, enabling us to teach using the connected learning that is so successful with girls. Children's literature proved to be a powerful context on which to build mathematical tasks and one that strongly influenced the development of children's perceptions about their world. We found the stories we read to children often became the essence of their reality.

This book-initiated reality is becoming increasingly important. In an age where children are more familiar with television characters than with their own grandparents and cousins, positive role models are in short supply. Mary Pipher, the author of *Reviving Ophelia*, states that at about age twelve, girls abandon their "self" and trade it for what they believe to be a culturally accepted version. This is particularly frightening considering the advertisements, MTV videos, and characters commonly found on television situation comedies. In 1992, researchers looked at the prototypical female as portrayed on television shows (Huston 1992). This female role model is young, beautiful, slim, and dependent on others. These are the very shows that are watched by both girls and boys on an average of six hours a day. It is not surprising then that girls idolize fashion models and are overly frustrated with their appearance while boys think girls are not capable of accomplishing much on their own.

Judy Mann, in her book about growing up female in America, puts it this way: "Little girls are so overwhelmed in this male culture that the story of little girls' lives is whispered, while the story of little boys' lives is shouted in books, movies, cartoons, and songs. We don't celebrate the wonderfulness of little girls nearly as much as we should" (1994, p. 19). As we approach the turn of the century, students need to read about and see in the media a more diverse pool of role models to act as mirrors so girls, in particular, can see reflections of their own selves in the real world. Unfortunately, we treat girls "like princesses when we want them to be presidents" (Shuker-Haines 1994, p. 76).

Our educational institutions mirror society in the learning girls experience. Although girls typically learn by making personal connections, in school settings they often face and are disadvantaged by separate, speedy, and silent learning (Gilligan, Lyons, and Hamner 1990). These factors are frequently mentioned as parts of the "disconnecting" girls encounter as they begin to lose their voice and change into the adolescents who claim that they "don't know."

Building a Model of Connected Teaching

Our goals in this action research are to bring powerful mathematics to females, to help them develop a clear conceptual understanding and passion for the subject, and to nurture independent learning skills that will translate into all aspects of their lives. Fifty years ago, 75 percent of what students needed to know on the job they had learned by the time they completed high school. Now that figure is 2 percent (Barth 1997). By blending girls' interest in reading with mathematics, by resisting dominant story lines and instead taking steps to use characters with hardy personalities, by encouraging independence and risk taking, and by developing significant mathematics, we hope to achieve these objectives.

The research-based strategies we suggest as particularly successful with females must be guided by the overall conceptions of teachers' views of the nature of mathematics and how it is learned. Adopting the techniques we speak of in isolation will not transform classroom practice. If manipulatives are used with a set of steps structured by the teacher to manipulate the materials, that experience will not compare to the learning achieved through student-driven exploration of concepts. Incorporating a prescribed use of materials will result in students merely being taught to memorize two procedures, one with materials, another with symbols. This rote use of materials leads to the lack of conceptual understanding we are trying to avoid. Also, if manipulatives are used but the boys handle the objects while the girls observe or record, traditional gender roles merely continue to be reinforced.

As a result, we generated and tested numerous mathematics lessons using books with hardy female characters in multiaged classrooms with seven- through eleven-year-olds. The activities are open in nature, have multiple entry levels, and lend themselves to use with several age groups and ability levels. We focused on the elementary years so that a strong base of confidence, perseverance, and motivation could be established.

Our belief is that there is a continuum, a full range of behaviors and actions with females and males distributed across the entire scope. Clearly, as many boys as girls will benefit from the support and suggestions we make and the exposure to multiple modes of knowing and models of understanding. As stated eloquently by Judy Mann, "We will never effectively change the way we raise girls unless we also change the way we raise boys, and we will never alter the outcome for most girls until we change the way boys think of girls" (1994, p. 15). In contrast to initial concerns, we found that boys in the class are just as interested in these stories as girls and both groups are making strides in mathematics achievement.

Seeking Stories

CHILDREN'S LITERATURE can transport young students to other worlds, places where there are possibilities and options that can be tried on for size. Like many quality books, these stories can be transformative and give girls an opportunity to test new versions of themselves. Therefore, our first goal was to select books that dealt with girls acting on their own initiative or through a web of connected relationships and support from others. This was not a simple process; finding books about strong female characters is not easy.

Many of the books selected are picture books, which is a strategic decision. Although some of these books are easy reading for upper elementary students, they often tell powerful tales in efficient ways with vivid visual clues that can be more easily integrated with mathematics lessons. They also are very effectively presented in two relatively brief readings, so the second reading can be scheduled just prior to the mathematical linkages.

When we introduced a piece of children's literature, we made it the focal point of our instructional time. In each case, we read the entire book with no interruptions. In the children's initial interaction with the text, the teachers encouraged them to open themselves to the literary experience. As the children discussed the qualities and personalities of the characters, they made connections between the characters' lives and their own.

We began the mathematics lessons with the second reading of a book. During this reading we asked the children, "What mathematics do you find in the story?" The children shared the mathematical wisdom they discovered in the story. Concentrating on the mathematics encouraged students to search throughout the book for mathematical ideas including vocabulary, problem solving, patterns, change, and skills in a real-world usage. Students became quite adept at finding examples of mathematics that may very likely escape the teacher's initial view or explanation.

The value of this second reading was to have children consider the story from another perspective as well as for another purpose. So, using literature with more subtle connections to mathematical ideas became a challenge. We are continually surprised and amazed by the number of ways the children noticed mathematics that we did not think about. These mathematical conversations invited children to piggyback on each other's thoughts, which we found generated a great deal of energy around "mathtalk."

Having read the story and identified the mathematical wisdom, we then introduced a prompt for a mathematical investigation or task. Of course, some of the initial prompts developed in advance of the reading are altered or even traded for other activities as a result of children's discussion and findings. The prompts connected the story lines about the hardy female characters with a problem-solving challenge. The tasks were purposely constructed to be open-ended to allow for multiple answers and multiple strategies.

The development of the prompt is a creative process that centers around engaging students in meaningful mathematical thinking with connections to the characters. Some might pose the question, "Why not just bypass the book and move directly to the math activity to save time?" Our research shows that by having a book and a character as a point of entry, you can always refer to the character or problem when assisting students as they forge forward in their own problem-solving process. The prompt is an initial catalyst to unify the group in their purpose and approach.

Connected Learning

One of the books used in the study was *Swamp Angel*, a Caldecott honor award-winning book by Anne Isaacs. In this book, the author spins a Tennessee folktale of Angelica Longrider, who at age twelve plucked a wagon train out of a marsh and was nicknamed Swamp Angel. When the call goes out across the land for someone to help rid the territory of a huge bear that is stealing the townspeople's food, Angelica is ready to try. After unsuccessful attempts by male competitors, Angelica rises to the challenge. The battle of strength and will lasts for days and nights, but Angelica succeeds and treats all of Tennessee and Kentucky to the bear feast.

The students found that thinking about what Angelica was able to do at a given age stirred their imagination. Contemplating what could be done if a person was two hundred feet tall encouraged everyone to fantasize. One child observed, "She would be the first one to know if it was going to rain, because she would feel it first." Another child saw a relationship between an investigation of the

Olympic Torch Relay and Swamp Angel's size and suggested that, "if she were running in the relay she would need to take only one step to go one kilometer."

Mathematical connections came about from the fact that Angelica was not like everyone else in size, strength, and skill. Discussions about the story led to thinking about measures of central tendency, as students gathered data about themselves and made comparisons. We introduced the mathematics prompt and it encouraged an exploration of what numerical data they would like to collect about children their age. Then students brainstormed questions, discussed possibilities, and came to consensus on what information they would like to discover. They decided to survey students ages nine through eleven and gather information on height, weight, shoe size, and hours of TV watched per day. Each student was responsible for collecting data on the four questions from twenty individuals within the designated age range. The students worked independently, gathering their data and compiling and averaging the information.

The teachers had previously introduced students to spreadsheets, and students decided that they wanted to put the survey information in this format. Students then designed a spreadsheet for use in organizing and analyzing the data (see Figure 7.1). The spreadsheet activity helped them recheck their data and gave students practice in developing appropriate formulas to calculate totals and the mean. One student explained, "We had to put formulas in the computer to get the average, the formula for weight, for example, =avg(C2..C21)."

Some students raised the question about what might be the response of students in other parts of the country. Using e-mail, students sent the survey questions to other parts of the country and Canada with the resulting information electronically returned to the class. These data were transferred to spreadsheets, and students compared and contrasted the averages in height, weight, shoe size, and hours of TV watched. Several mathematical activities emerged as a result of the e-mail data. The measurements sent from other schools did not always come in inches, and some classes reported in decimal form while others used fractions. This was a teachable moment. Our students also had an opportunity to place their class's numerical data side by side with a class from another city and write mathematical

	A	B	C	D	E
1	NAME	HEIGHT	WEIGHT	SHOE SIZE	HRS. TV
2	Rhonisha	56	110	8	2
3	Kristy	56	75	5.5	6
4	Lori	50	68	5.5	1
5	Ginny	56	64	4	3
6	Tonya	58	80	6.5	3.5
7	Ali	56	69	3.5	1
8	Emily	61	80	8	1
9	Lauren	56	80	3.5	3
10	Eric	58	70	4	5
11	Amber	60	70	7	1
12	Alisha	53	47	1.5	4
13	Jessica	61	80	7	1
14	Freddie	67	70	5	3
15	J.W.	58	75	6	5
16	Angelique	60	75	6	5
17	Mike	57	72	6	3
18	Nicole	53	70	8.5	1
19	Danyell	58	69	4.5	3
20	Lawrence	53	70	4	3
21	Allison	56	69	3.5	1
22	AVERAGE	57.15	73.15	5.375	2.775
23					
24					

Figure 7.1 Swamp Angel random survey.

conjectures about the comparisons. A child wrote, "The tallest and shortest came from the other class [New York] data." In looking at other comparisons a student wrote, "For example our average height was 56.35 [inches] and theirs was 59 so that proves that they were taller. The average shoe size was 5.8 but the other class average was 6.1, so that meant they also had bigger feet." Another child summarized her data in the following way: "We found out the average fourth grader watches 3 hours of TV a day, has a shoe size of about 5, weighs 76.75 pounds and their height is 56 inches."

Students then decided to actually use the data to create a "real" version of AverageKid. Using a roll of brown paper they took the average measurements already collected to help them form the prototypical student. They started by marking off the height and then tried to find someone the exact weight of 76.75 pounds. Then they realized that although the person was the correct weight they were smaller in height. When the person lay down on the paper the group realized that the proportion would not be accurate. When they found a closer match in height and weight to the statistics, they traced the body estimating a little more weight in some places. The shoe size was added when they again found a child with an exact match. Some children wanted to add other data, so they found the average pulse rate in the class and added that number to a heart-shaped outline on the AverageKid's chest. Of course it was interesting to them that although this was the average child, none of the children in the class actually had all of the average characteristics. The concrete version of the data helped some children see connections that they had not made before.

The students wrote reflectively on what they found about students in their corner of the world from interpreting their survey data. This activity linked well with the NCTM Standard of Communication that suggests students should realize that representing, discussing, reading, writing, and listening to mathematics are vital parts of their lives.

Since the children are in the multiage classes for more than one year, this activity began at the end of one school year and awaited the children at the beginning of the next year. Throughout the investigation and data collection, the teacher kept questioning the students about who would like to know this data. Who would be interested in shoe sizes, height, weight, and TV watching in different parts of the continent? Students considered whether this information might be valuable in marketing products to people their age. The consensus came down to several groups that might be able to use the findings, including shoe companies, clothing companies, and television producers. Then students wrote letters to these groups regarding the implications of the survey results.

Angelica Longrider was a risk taker. Her example led the class on a continentwide search for data on how the students compared with other nine-, ten-, and eleven-year-olds. Her "hardy personality" left us with an avenue to grow more knowledgeable about our world and ourselves.

Concluding Thoughts

We are pleased that our action research helped us poke holes in some of the myths about females' mathematics performance. In reality, girls can be successful in mathematics while building confidence. Many teachers recognize that they can become too protective in an effort to shield girls from failure. It is the subtle rather than the overt behaviors that should be unmasked and counteracted.

The media and society will continue to discourage females in mathematics-related activities. Therefore, teachers and parents must end the silence. They should not fail to encourage girls to be risk takers, problem solvers, and logical thinkers. As adapted from *Growing Smart: What's Working for Girls in School* (1995), the American Association of University Women suggests educators, parents, and communities work together to create programs that: celebrate girls' strong identity; respect girls as central players; connect girls to caring adults; ensure girls' participation and success; and empower girls to realize their dreams. "Gender equity is about enriching classrooms, widening opportunities, and expanding choices for *all* students. The notion that helping girls means injuring boys amounts to a defense of a status quo that we all know is serving too few of our students well. Surely it is as important for boys to learn about the contributions of women to our nation as it is for girls to study this information" (Bailey 1996, pp. 75–76).

We are seeking ways to eliminate the roadblocks and hurdles that limit the options for both sexes. Currently, males can look at what either males or females are doing and feel fully able to attack similar situations. On the other hand, females often perceive only what they see other females doing as being a possibility for them. If teachers wish to develop the underlying traits that strengthen the problem-solving abilities of females, they need to look at ways to introduce female characters with hardy personalities into their instruction. As we seek ways to help create more equitable classrooms we find the means of helping all students become mathematically literate. Perhaps through continued investigation of links between "feisty-female" characters in stories and mathematics concepts a solution can be identified.

References

American Association of University Women (AAUW). 1995. *Growing Smart: What's Working for Girls in School.* Washington, DC: AAUW Foundation.

Bailey, S. 1996. Shortchanging Girls and Boys. *Educational Leadership* 53, 8: 75–79.

Barth, R. 1997. The Leader as Learner. *Education Week* 56 (March 5): 42.

Gilligan, Carol, Nona P. Lyons, and Trudy Hamner, eds. 1990. *Making Connections: The Relational World of Adolescent Girls at Emma Willard School.* Cambridge, MA: Harvard University Press.

Huston, A. C. 1992. *Big World, Small Screen: The Role of TV in American Society.* Lincoln, NE: University of Nebraska Press.

Isaacs, A. 1994. *Swamp Angel.* New York: Dutton.

Karp, Karen, E. Todd Brown, Linda Allen, and Candy Allen. 1998. *Feisty Females: Inspiring Girls to Think Mathematically.* Portsmouth, NH: Heinemann.

Mann, J. 1994. *The Difference: Growing Up Female in America.* New York: Warner.

Ouellette, S. K., and M. Puccetti. 1983. Personality and Social Resources in Stress Resistance. *Journal of Personality and Social Psychology* 45: 839–850.

Pipher, Mary. 1994. *Reviving Ophelia: Saving the Selves of Adolescent Girls.* New York: Putnam.

Shuker-Haines, F. 1994. On the Home Front. *Parenting* (April): 75–76.

Tar Baby

Khalilah Joseph

During the Atlantic slave trade, Africans on plantations across the South were treated like animals. They were thought to be less than human, but even within this undignified category, they were further classified by color. It started that far back: When all blacks were nothing, still color was an issue. The lighter you were, the closer to the house you toiled. In those days, there was no beauty in color, and if you had some, you were destined to be working way out in the field. Even today, I see the remnants of the Field nigga, House nigga syndrome.

It happens in a continuous motion through music videos, movies, magazines, and daily life. I can watch a video by a given artist and before the end of it, the object of desire will prance across the screen, and, of course, she'll be a honey-dipped, barely-brown bombshell.

In the movie *Waiting to Exhale,* a film targeted at African American women, the lightest woman in the movie was the male magnet. And the dark skin sister? It took her the whole movie just to get a date. Women of color are greatly downsized in the movies. Angela Bassett could be a battered wife, but could she be a *Pretty Woman* or be the object of an *Indecent Proposal?*

In most magazines you pick up, you can find at least one African American woman, but usually she is a little light-eyed biracial girl who does little to represent women of color. Be gone with those tiny-waisted, no-hip-having heifers. Bring on the models who range in color from caramel to dark chocolate. Then give them features familiar to Negro women. I'm talking about big booties, child-bearing hips, thunder thighs.

As a dark-skinned girl, I was ridiculed. I can remember a time when one of my elementary school classes had a career fair. Like many other girls my age, I wanted to be an actress or a model. My classmates made it painfully clear that dark-skinned girls are not considered pretty. They couldn't imagine why I would think that I could become a model. They suggested that I be a nurse or a teacher. I was called names like "tar baby" or "blackie." As a young girl I couldn't understand why some people of my own race would tease me about something I could not change.

As women of color we have made progress: we are teachers, lawyers, doctors. We are elected to office. Who knows, maybe one day, we dark-skinned women will be video hoochies, too.

8

Worth Waiting For: Girls Writing for Their Lives in the Bronx

Jennifer Tendero

the Bronx—a complex identity built on a reputation of being tough and resilient—they tell me the school is the only thing in their neighborhood they're proud of, and I can understand this.

On our way to lunch at El Loco Taco one day, Nina pointed out the "pharmacists" who do business in her apartment building. "There is a courtyard in the middle [of my building], but everyone knows you only go in it to get drugs or get raped," she said matter-of-factly. Her neighborhood was recently cited in the *New York Times* as the most dangerous [police] precinct in the city, due to an increase in homicides and strained relations between law enforcement and the people who live there.

Yet it's neither fair nor accurate to overlook the sense of community that pervades the area. I'm just beginning to learn the dynamics of the families I serve, but I do know that raising a child seems to be an act that includes everyone, even my students, who often come to our afterschool tutoring program toting their younger siblings.

The Authors Workshop consists of 70 percent Latinos and 30 percent Blacks. Ninety-nine percent of our students qualify for a free lunch. In 1996 I.S. 306 was officially named an SURR school—a School Under Research and Review—by the New York State Board of Education, due to its extremely low reading and math scores. There were only nine other schools in the entire state of New York with scores as low as ours. There was, and is, great administrative pressure to improve the test scores in order to avoid being taken over by the state. This was the highly charged climate I stepped into when I accepted a job teaching eighth-grade English, Social Studies, and Community Service for my second year of teaching.

I began the year by inviting fourteen eighth-grade girls in on a yearlong conversation about teen pregnancy. It was scary and tentative and the best invitation I ever gave. In a neighborhood where teenage pregnancy is a ubiquitous rite of passage for many girls, and in a school that values inquiry and preaches the power of literacy, it was the only thing to do given the school's situation that September.

We began the year by reading Sandra Cisneros' *The House on Mango Street* and by writing growing-up stories, stories of our neighborhood, and vignettes about the streets on which we lived. As a new teacher in the Write for Your Life project, I knew I wanted to set the curricular stage, as it were, for students to reflect on their community through reading and writing. My invitation to them was deliberate. I wanted to open up a dialogic curriculum in my class, in which my students and I shaped the curriculum through our mutual inquiry.

Patricia Stock developed this pedagogy as the basis for a case study of a classroom in Saginaw, Michigan, in her book *The Dialogic Curriculum*. This pedagogy, in contrast to what Friere (1970) called the "banking concept" of education, in which students are seen as reception sites for the knowledge that teachers deposit into them, demands that students actively participate in their education (Stock 1995). It is not an occasion for the teacher to bow out, but an opportunity for students to discover an authentic topic of inquiry that they want to study. Every successful Write for Your Life classroom I'd seen had at its core student-initiated and teacher-facilitated inquiry, which directly led to social action via literacy. In order for our particular Community Service class to work well, I believed it was imperative that our curriculum emerge from student inquiry as well.

Over the next few weeks, as we traveled down Mango Street, I began writing workshop with a whole-group exercise of asking students to share what they were writing. "Violence. My aunt was killed last year," said one student. "Gangs." "Drugs." These might seem like viable urban themes flowing with enough rich possibilities to consume the most industrious students indefinitely. They are. Considering that 306 is on the cusp of the South Bronx, a place of de facto segregation, the poorest congressional district in the United States, and home of notorious violence, it is not surprising that these were themes of my students' lives. I did not want to be flippant about the problems that pressed upon these kids, but I did want to tackle something they could change by their reading and writing.

I challenged my students to find subthemes in their writing. I told them, "Sometimes writers use one theme—death, for example—to write about and explore loneliness or loss. In order to discover the themes in your writing, you will have to go below the surface of your words. Jot down in the margins of your paper all the subthemes or issues you can find in your writing."

What they found there were fears, wonderings, secrets. Your body changing. Teens in life. Growing up in your neighborhood. How you dress in school and how it affects you. Having babies. Miracles. Real, and possibly deeper, issues in their lives were emerging. I hoped we could find something that would engage us in a collective inquiry. Three days later, we did.

As I conferred during writing workshop with students about the pieces they wanted to publish, I noticed that Felice was revising an opinion piece on the irresponsibility of some teen mothers, and Tasha was working with Teah and Yolanda on a play that revolved around a teenager who gets pregnant. I had just had a conversation with Julia and Yvonta in which they said, "Kids grow up so fast nowadays. It seems like one minute you're playing those [childhood] games and the next you're pregnant and all grown up!"

It seemed that the girls might benefit from working together as they wrote, bouncing ideas off one another and forming a sort of informal inquiry group on the topic of teen pregnancy. I told them what I was thinking, and the girls, who were not all friends, seemed hesitant but game.

After they pushed their desks together, I asked them, "Is teenage pregnancy a problem in this community?" "Yes!" they replied emphatically. What followed was a barrage of stories about sisters, friends, and cousins who were pregnant or already mothers.

"My brother told me that they're handing out condoms for free on the corner of Davison and Tremont," said Benita.

"Yeah, they can hand out all the condoms they want," said Julia, "but facts is facts. Girls are still getting pregnant all over the place."

"Mmm-hmm, and their mothers are the ones stuck caring for the babies," added Felice.

I heard in their conversation a strong desire not to be like that, mixed with a wariness that their future careened in that direction anyway. This exchange raised a couple of key questions for me: would it be possible to critically examine the phenomenon of teen pregnancy with these eighth graders, and how could studying this issue benefit the community around us? Teen pregnancy was clearly not a problem easily solved with the distribution of birth control. Rather, it was, as the girls implied, a complex issue. What if I could, in Freire's words, re-present it not as a lecture, but as a problem? If teenage pregnancy were an epidemic that could be diminished by teachers and parents lecturing to adolescents, it would have been wiped out long ago. But it seems that a solution must be found in the midst of dialogue and would include teenagers naming and owning teen pregnancy as a real and solvable problem in their lives.

The next time we had workshop, I asked that same group if they wanted to study the issue of teen pregnancy in Community Service class. They did, quickly passing around a sign-up sheet to see how many people were interested in joining them. I returned to school two days later after attending a conference and found on my desk a typed proposal written by two female students to Kim Parreres and AnneMarie Parrotta, the directors of Authors Workshop, asking to use the kitchen for one period each Tuesday and Thursday for meetings in which to talk about and study the problem of teen pregnancy in our community. I was stunned at their quick action. In the space of three days, the invitation had been responded to and the TEEN Group had formed. They were shifting from writing about their lives to writing for their lives. Two things occurred to me when I saw the proposal sitting on my desk: this was clearly something they wanted to study, and it would sustain itself if and because they felt passionately about it. The typed proposal, the naming of a group, and the request for a space of their own in which to study teen pregnancy, was all their own doing.

Reflecting on the year always humbles me, teaches me how much there is to learn. I ought to expect the world from my students, yet eighth graders are a volatile bunch, quickly changing allegiances and interests. I underestimate them at times. The societal expectation of failure that so bombards my kids was present in their own teacher, and though I was thrilled that the group was forming, I didn't think it would go where it did, and for so long. That it did is testimony to the power of genuine, student-initiated inquiry, and how it affects kids' lives.

Trust

The investigation will be impossible without a relation of mutual understanding and trust . . . trust is established by dialogue.

PAULO FREIRE, *Pedagogy of the Oppressed*

WE HAD the first TEEN Group meeting. Fourteen girls and I met in the empty school kitchen. The boys weren't interested in attending. The girls appointed Julia the leader of the TEEN Group. Julia has two sisters, ages seventeen and nineteen, who are both teen mothers. At our first meeting she said, "If anyone thinks they want a baby now, come over to my house and spend just one day with my two nieces! I've seen how much work they are, and I'm telling you, I'm waiting a long time before I have one of my own. Sure, they're cute, and my sisters are both gonna graduate from high school, but they've had to switch to a special school so they can take the girls, and they can't go out to parties like they used to. It's not as easy as it looks."

Nearly all the girls in my class were born when their mothers were teenagers, but I think Julia's daily proximity to two teen mothers gave her, in the girls' minds, extra authority on teen pregnancy that they didn't have. A willowy Latina with long, brown hair and a very wide smile, Julia is arguably the prettiest girl in the whole eighth grade. Her long nails rap delicately on the desk when she is stuck on a line of poetry. She is a voracious writer who put together a typed portfolio of one hundred of her best poems to take with her to a high school interview. Her reputation for being smart and fair made her the most popular girl in our class. It made sense for her to be the leader of the group.

During the first few meetings, the girls seemed shy around each other, preferring to exchange stories of cousins, aunts, and friends who were teen mothers. I felt it was important for the girls to connect with each other, to realize shared experiences. They needed to know that the group was a safe place for them, and early on, the girls agreed that everything said in the kitchen would stay there.

"It won't work if we can't trust each other. We got to stick close this year. We're all gonna hear things in this group that we can't tell nobody else, not even your friends in other classes, okay?" said Julia. (As far as I know, this happened only once, when Tess was heard telling Kaylie, who chose not to be in the TEEN Group, something about one of the girls. She was promptly kicked out of the group. After a little mediation and an apology, she was grudgingly let back in.)

From October to December, the girls engaged in a dialogue that at times resembled a TV talk show. It was frustrating but necessary, I think, to give the girls the space to build mutual understanding and trust. Though we directed the discussions at times, and pushed the girls to think critically about teen pregnancy, we worked at being patient with both their process of inquiry and their need to establish trust with dialogue.

Boundaries

What do you do in there, anyway?

LUPE, *one of the boys in my class*

IT WAS a legitimate question. Each week fourteen girls left Room 304, traipsed down the hall, and disappeared into the school kitchen, closing the door behind them. After a disastrous coed meeting early on, the girls decided that only girls would be in the TEEN Group.

What happened in that meeting made me reconsider one of Gloria Steinem's thoughts on education: Girls learn better with girls and boys learn better with girls. Girls who had spoken freely in other TEEN Group meetings were absolutely silenced in the presence of only two boys, who vied for attention by jumping out of their seats and waving their hands wildly in the air. In preparation for the meeting the girls had read an article Tony had found and copied. The boys, who had not read the article, repeatedly insisted on answering the questions that Julia raised about it, and most of the girls sat in their seats with their hands in their laps. A few tried to talk, but it was a frustrating meeting in which little was accomplished. I asked the girls to meet with me for a few minutes before lunch.

"How do you think the meeting went?" I asked.

"Not so good," said Keanna.

"I didn't like having the boys there," said Felice. "It was like, different than when we just met with the girls. I don't know, I just liked it better the way it was."

"That's what I think, too," I said. "You know, sometimes it's better for girls to have a space of their own where they can meet and talk without boys. What I saw today is that most of you who normally talk during TEEN Group didn't talk at all when the boys were there. That concerns me."

Of course I was appalled at what had happened during that meeting, and embarrassed at my own ignorance of the boys' domination in my classroom. I'm a strong woman, yet I allowed the same glaringly unfair gender roles to exist in my classroom in the Bronx as my teachers had when I was a junior high school student in Michigan.

I had never before considered what a vital and rich environment might be created when girls learned with each other, without boys. My experiences with the TEEN Group pushed me, as a beginning teacher-researcher, to look at how my students learn best, and with whom. I'm convinced the girls of the TEEN Group learned best apart from the boys. Girls who were flirtatious and scattered in our classroom were consistently focused during TEEN Group meetings. The contrast in their behavior is too obvious to ignore, and it intrigues me enough that I continue to wonder how I can provide my students with an environment that will best nurture their learning.

No boys allowed, the girls decided, except Tony and Dave, who would provide resources through Write for Your Life and act as university researchers.

With that decided, the shape of our meetings was set. One of us adults attended each meeting in which the girls read articles they or Tony found, or that Dave had pulled off the Web. They struggled through everything from the *Chicago Tribune*'s survey, "Teenage Girls Talk About Pregnancy," to "Adolescent Pregnancy: A Preventable Consequence" by Barbara and Ray Yawn (an article written by doctors for doctors), to *Teen Pregnancy Facts,* a report collected for the NAEHA task force. Sometimes the group spent an entire meeting decoding complex writing.

There was a clear pattern to their meetings, which often began with the girls going over pieces of writing they had done. They were constantly collaborating as they revised stories, poems, and plays that centered around teenage pregnancy or reviewed articles they had read for that day. Julia usually brought questions for discussion to the meetings, neatly written under the day's agenda in the TEEN Group's journal: Is it true that your life changes after you have a child? What do you lose from having a child? Tony, David, and I would collaborate with her before the meetings, finding out what she wanted to accomplish that day and laying out tentative plans for future meetings.

By giving the girls choices of what they studied and how the TEEN Group meetings ran, I was hoping they would feel more responsibility and choice in their lives. Part of the tension for me of student-led and student-initiated inquiry is in determining when I should step in as a leader and when I need to blend into the group. This was complicated by my being an older white female, and, as such, outside the peer group. Though we had a solid relationship, there was a solidarity among the girls of which I was not a part. Because I was their teacher, I had a responsibility to guide their inquiry into helpful directions. When they wanted to know more about abortion, I was honest with them and said that I didn't feel comfortable exploring abortion with a group of fourteen-year-olds whose goal was to prevent teen pregnancy, but I did show them where they could get more information in the yellow pages. When there were personality conflicts, I insisted on mediating and solving the problem with them before the next meeting.

Sometimes Julia led the group so flawlessly that I could do nothing else but step back, amazed. When the girls' passion was channeled into serious inquiry that pushed them to rearrange their conception of teenage pregnancy and propelled them to envision their lives as ones filled with possibilities, the TEEN Group was at its best.

Critical Interventions

The oppressed (who do not commit themselves to the struggle unless they are convinced, and who, if they do not make such a commitment, withhold the indispensable conditions for this struggle) must reach this conviction as subjects, not objects. They must intervene critically in the situation which surrounds them and whose mark they bear.

PAULO FREIRE, *Pedagogy of the Oppressed*

IN DECEMBER, with our help, the girls decided they would write a grant proposal to the Write for Your Life foundation to secure funds to purchase a common text they could read and discuss together. Their final project would take the form of a booklet of their writing and research on teenage pregnancy that they would pass out to the community. These were decisions to use their literacy to take social action in the communities of the TEEN Group and their neighborhood.

The girls chose two books to read about teenage pregnancy. For three weeks they had read the books and reviewed them in the group, passing them around for everyone to read. These students, who had scored so low on the New York State Reading Test the previous year, literally mobbed David when he brought them books to review, quickly dog-earing and reading them incessantly, even during lunch.

Tony worked on the practicalities of grant writing with a committee of girls from the TEEN Group for most of December. By mid-January, the grant proposal was mailed out to Write for Your Life classrooms around the country, where it was evaluated by students, teachers, and administrators. A few weeks later, Tony presented the girls with a letter written on behalf of Write for Your Life, stating they'd been awarded the grant they had requested. Getting the grant was possibly the first time these teenagers from the Bronx had seen their literacy work for them in such a real and positive way.

"I never thought that you could just get money like that by doing research," said Felice. It is unusual for eighth graders to write grant proposals. Unusual, but not impossible. The girls were teaching me that there were more possibilities than I had imagined.

But we had neglected to check if we could get the books they chose. After numerous book searches, we discovered the books they'd requested were recently out of print, and we couldn't find fourteen copies of each. So the girls began again the process of reading and reviewing books. Finally, they chose a nonfiction book called *Surviving Teen Pregnancy,* by Shirley Arthur.

"This book doesn't seem to have a lot to do with preventing teen pregnancy," we adults questioned. "But we've already read a lot of the prevention stuff," Yolanda explained for the group, "and now we want to see what the other side of teen pregnancy is like. We're still for preventing it, but we need to look at this, too." We could have pushed them to choose another book, but they were right. They had the right to peek into how others have survived teenage pregnancy.

In the middle of reading the book, the girls decided to interview Julia's sister and her friend, ages seventeen and fifteen, about their experiences as teen mothers. Tony helped them organize their questions. At the three-hour interview, both mothers candidly admitted they had wanted to get pregnant.

"Oh, I wanted a baby so bad," said Bettina, "but honestly, if I could do it again, I'd wait, because there ain't nothing I can do by myself no more. I always got my son to take care of. I love my baby, don't get me wrong, but I should've waited."

They're becoming convinced, I thought during the interview. The girls had researched how teen pregnancy negatively affects young mothers and society, they had read stories written by and about teen mothers who struggle so hard to make it as single parents, they had been the product of teen pregnancies, and they had even tried being mothers themselves. Now they were hearing it from girls only a few years older than themselves: wait.

Writing New Lives

It was after that interview that the girls began to define their futures by declaring how old they wanted to be before having sex. I'm waiting until I get married to have kids, they said. Felice talked about which college she wanted to attend. I felt the momentum that is born out of conviction and determination begin to surface in the group. The girls were ready to intervene critically in the situation which surrounds them.

Shortly after the interview, the girls decided it was time to publish the booklet. Since they had been writing about teenage pregnancy the whole year and had written stories and poems from the interview with the teen mothers, there was a wealth of writing from which to choose for publication. Tony and David recruited some of their students from Teachers College to help with final editing and typing, and they were invaluable to us on an especially frenetic day in June when we all worked in a hot, stuffy room for seven hours straight, editing and typing, finally collapsing at 2:30 in the afternoon to consume take-out pizza and toast our joint efforts with warm pop sloshing in plastic cups.

The forty-page booklet of stories and poems about waiting, warning, survival, and growing up—peppered with facts the girls had learned in their research and even a quiz titled, Are You Ready to Have Sex?—was titled *Our So-Called Teen Years*. It was distributed to students in our school, community health clinics, local and state politicians, and Write for Your Life classrooms around the country.

The collaboration between the middle school and university was invigorating. In June, Tony invited the TEEN Group to speak to the students in his Adolescent Literature class at the Teachers College. As we rode the subway from the Bronx to the other world of Columbia University and Manhattan, I marveled at the poise of the girls sitting around me. Through their research and reading they had become knowledgeable not only about teen pregnancy but also about the process of forming a group to study a problem and working toward making it better. Undeniably oppressed economically, politically, and socially, these girls had done the hard work necessary to intervene critically in their own situation, and had earned an invitation to a graduate classroom in an Ivy League university to share what they had learned with preservice teachers.

Someone at both that visit and the publication party asked the girls to sum up what they'd learned in the TEEN Group. Vivian said,

"We learned we're worth waiting for." And that's it, I think. The suspicion that there is something else beyond the narrow reality you live in, choices you hadn't even imagined, is enough to keep you up nights and sustain your interest for ten months.

For their final project, all my English students had to conduct research to answer questions they had. One night as I was responding to them, Tony and I noticed something different about the papers written by the girls in the TEEN Group: every girl in that group except two chose to answer a question about her career. Julia asked, What kind of writer do I want to become? Felice's question was, What is the best medical school for me to attend? Yolanda wanted to know what kind of artist she should be, and Zarah's research helped her decide what type of law she might practice someday. One after another they had discovered possibilities they thought were unattainable, and in the process of gathering reasons for not becoming teenage mothers, their earlier wariness that their future careened in that direction anyway fell away.

Though they live in the same neighborhood, the girls are going to different high schools throughout the city. We've agreed to meet a few times a year over dinner. They met with the group of sixth graders I'll have next year and passed the torch over to them to sustain and elaborate on the work they did this year. That is hopeful to me—true community service. I don't know what choices the girls will make beyond middle school, but I do know that within my hope that they'll see all the possibilities and make prudent ones, lies the conviction that for most of the girls, the work they did this past year will be a powerful force in how they live their lives. I carry their words from the preface to *Our So-Called Teen Years* with me always:

Our lives are ours and our teen years are some of the most memorable. If you get pregnant or if you get someone pregnant, they become your so-called teen years.

As you read this booklet, there will be a lot of messages and stories to help you realize that life is too precious to waste. Having a childhood is more important than having a child and experiencing an adult lifestyle too soon.

We have put a lot of effort and all of our hopes into this booklet. We would like teenagers everywhere to read this booklet and take it as a wake-up call in life.

References

Freire, Paulo. 1970. *Pedagogy of the Oppressed*. New York: Continuum.

Stock, Patricia. 1995. *The Dialogic Curriculum*. Portsmouth, NH: Boynton/Cook.

9

"I Believe in Myself": The Theories of Immigrant Girls

Kiran Dilip Purohit

I WENT to lunch with a group of students and another teacher one Saturday afternoon. We had spent the morning working in a park near our school in Manhattan's Chinatown, and we were pleased to relax at last in the cool dining room of a Vietnamese restaurant. After the initial excitement of reading the menu and ordering—most of the Chinese students had never tried Vietnamese food—we began to chat while we waited for lunch. We talked about different things until one girl turned to me and asked, "Ms. Purohit, what do you *believe*?" Everyone was listening for my answer, but I wasn't even sure what she meant, so I turned the question on my student. "I'm not sure what you mean. What do *you* believe?" "Well, I mean like praying," she replied. "My family believes in Buddhism." A couple of students nodded in agreement, and one by one they offered an explanation of what their family practices. "Buddhism." "I don't know." "We pray to Allah." "Nothing." "My family goes to church." Last in the circle, the girl seated across from me—a sixth grader whom I had taught for most of the year—said simply, "I believe in myself." The others at the table nodded seriously, respectfully.

I always think of this moment as I try to make my work as a science teacher meaningful for the middle schoolers in my classroom. Teaching people with backgrounds so different from my own—virtually all my students are Chinese, many of them recent immigrants—I am always faced with contradictions and surprises as I try to make sense of where they are coming from. I know something, from experience, of what it's like to go through middle school and to try to succeed in school. I know about the obstacles girls face, especially in math and science, as they move into high school and college courses. But it is a daily challenge to understand what the girls in my class bring to school. On the one hand, the prevailing image of Asian girls, and one which I encounter often in my classroom, is deferential, cautious silence. They speak in soft voices and lean in close when speaking to each other. Their comments in class seem hesitant and measured. On the other hand, as the lunchtime conversation above typifies, these girls are powerful and independent. Many of them work in garment factories with their mothers, or are responsible for several younger siblings in addition to their schoolwork; moreover, they have negotiated a move from homes in China to the dynamic confusion of Chinatown.

I, and other teachers, often focus on the first part of this characterization of the girls in my classroom: the overwhelming silence. In an effort to help girls find and develop their voices in English, we tell them to speak up in class. Or we may encourage them to work silently by rewarding the diligent desk work at which many silent students excel. In either case, the emphasis is on the way students do or do not speak. My conversations with girls from my classes have reminded me how one-sided it is always to combat the students' silence. Instead of focusing on the ways in which girls in my classroom lack the voice to speak up in English, how can I instead examine what they *don't* lack? What can I learn from these girls about schools and classrooms? In this chapter I will tell about the insights, thoughts, and theories of middle school girls who are recent immigrants and whom I taught or met at school. My aim was to discover how I could make these girls' voices "heard" in my science classroom, not just through tricks and exercises but through changing the ways we together create a scientific community in the classroom to include many voices. Learning with my students—hearing their beliefs and perspectives—has helped me to do this.

The designation of "ESL" is a dubious one to assign to any student. In the context of my school, ESL is a misnomer; nearly everyone fits that description. ESL and its slimy brother LEP (Limited English Proficiency) are arbitrary acronyms used to group and sort children—who are more different than alike in reading ability, native language writing skills, family background, English speaking ability, and countless other ways—based on standardized test scores. The label "ESL," which accurately indicates that certain students are learning the English language, only points to the extreme diversity in the class. When teaching classes designated LEP or ESL I try to allow for each student's individuality rather than be bound by contrived similarities.

In addition to finding the time to talk with students during classes, I also found it necessary to structure outside time to talk in smaller groups with girls I was teaching. I suspected these girls had much to say, but we simply lacked the time in the school day to share stories. One afternoon on a trip with another teacher and just a few students, a girl from one of my classes began to tell me the story of how she came to New York. She told me about living most of her childhood separate from her parents, as they wanted a son but could not have a second child under China's one-child laws. She told me about another sister who was still in China, and about the one-bedroom apartment her family shared with two other families. I realized that I, as a teacher, had a lot to understand and that these students had much that they could explain to me, given the time and the occasion to do so.

Having arrived in Chinatown in the past two to four years, students learned to make sense of the world in terms they may not have previously known. My students have made sense of a new neighborhood, a new language, and a new, huge school serving around 1500 students. Their comments about the school and life in the city reflect thought and great effort to understand a new place.

It is all too easy, however, to forget how much they have learned and assimilated, as those who are learning English struggle to communicate their observations. For instance, in a conversation with several students, Jenny was explaining to me an odd classroom dynamic of having many boys and only a few girls—the situation in her sixth-grade class.

I think maybe the girls think that the boys are too much in the class, so work harder than them. . . . Sometimes, I think my class has too many boys. Um, I think it's, um, we have half the boys' number of the girls, so the girls think that, maybe people think that more people can work better, so we girls have to feel . . . we want to . . . we have to work hard, more harder than before.

Jenny is explaining a sentiment shared by all kinds of folks who feel that they have to work twice as hard to get noticed in their work simply because they are in the minority or are judged to be less qualified. I am struck both by the profound nature of this thought—and by how long it took Jenny to say it. Perhaps the single most important step toward discovering the theories of girls lies simply in giving them the time and space to speak freely and in recognizing that each child has her own voice.

Many students struggle to find their voices through renaming themselves. In my first few weeks teaching, I quickly discovered that I had not only to learn the unfamiliar Chinese names of all my students, but also the American names they chose—even *new* American names they took on during the year. A friend compared the experience to reading Dostoevsky: without any knowledge of what was going on, the naming and renaming seemed to me arbitrary and capricious. The Chinese name "Long Lan" became the American-sounding "Lana," only to metamorphose further to "Lani." What a strange denial of Chinese identity I thought this was!

Then one day near the end of the year a student named Xiao Yu Liang started writing on her papers "Serena (Xiao Yu) Liang." I asked if she preferred to be called "Serena," and she told me yes, that she had chosen this name. I still had trouble, however, remembering the switch every time we talked, and at best I called her "Serena" half the time. I realized how much thought it takes to change one's name—and how much consideration had obviously gone into Xiao Yu's deciding she preferred to be identified as "Serena." Similarly for a student who refuses to change her name, the decision requires a great deal of thought and justification.

Names like Jenny, Mandy, Kimberly, or Daisy are, in America, a little less unusual than Serena, but adopting these identities carries great significance for students who are new Americans. Deciding on a different name, learning and thinking about different possibilities, is a quiet and strong statement about who we are. Even I have puzzled about how I want my students to address me; I frequently change my mind about what I want to be called. Many students, like Xiao Yu (Serena), remain ambivalent about the switch and express pride in their Chinese name. When I asked a student named Kelly, a name she picked from the dictionary, why she had "changed her name," she was shocked. She patiently explained that she had *not* changed her name. "My name is the *same*," she pointed out. "In Chinese, we put the family name first, so I still have the same name." I said that some people still might think she had changed her name, since everyone calls her Kelly, but she insisted she had not, and that it made sense. "It's America. I need an American name!" she repeated to me. But Kelly writes her Chinese name in parentheses on all her papers.

In a beautiful piece called "My Name," a student named Yan E wrote of this ambivalence and of how her identity and her place as an American are connected to her name. She remembers stories unique to her childhood in China, yet she seriously considers the difficulty that her unusual Chinese name makes so apparent:

My parents told me in Chinese my name mean hot, fire to hurt, I think it means I have a bad health and get sick very often. In English my name mean pretty or nice. This sounds good to me, but still it is very strange in my middle name, because it is only a letter E.

. . . The first name mean that I born on a hot day in March. My uncle said I should have a soft name, not too strong. Because he think all women are weak. I don't think so. Some women are stronger than some men.

In the United States Public Elementary School when I just came, all the kids in my class think I have a funny name. Some people teased me because I don't know any English. After many days they stopped teasing me because more new students are coming, and they all have Chinese names like mine. I felt a lot more comfortable.

Most of the time I feel my name is more strange than my friends, because of my middle name only one letter, they don't have any name that's only one letter, I want to change my name, but I don't like any English name, because most of the name a lot people already have. Beside my own name make me feel more like myself, so I like it and I will never change.

The complex identity of these girls is vividly expressed by their choosing new names while retaining the old ones in parentheses. They are not simply adolescent girls trying to make their way through middle school, just as they are not only immigrant Chinese children striving to assimilate. If I am going to understand what they bring to school and what they hold as important, my teaching has to begin with this *complexity*. As Judith Butler warns us, broad attempts to address the politics of gender must not arise out of simplifying the other kinds of identity girls and women have. "Perhaps also part of what dialogic understanding entails is the acceptance of divergence, breakage, splinter, and fragmentation as part of the often tortuous process of democratization" (1990, pp. 14–15). Instead of doubting the validity of certain aspects of students' cultural life and holding up certain others, we teachers must accommodate even the most complex facets of the children we teach if we are to do our jobs well.

This process of coming to understand students better is not an "extra" in the education of girls. Teaching must incorporate a struggle to work *with* students as they learn about English or become Americans or understand the way the school works. We cannot teach girls in a way that really gets at their questions in science or any other subject until we understand what those questions are. In the words of Paulo Freire (1970), "Education must begin with the solution of the teacher-student contradiction, by reconciling the poles of the contradiction so that both are simultaneously teachers *and* students" (p. 53).

Moreover, we cannot leave the cultures of our students out of classroom dialogue, most simply because we cannot expect students to leave their culture at home. On the contrary, the girls from my class were acutely aware of the place they were expected to hold as Chinese girls and as children growing up in Chinatown. These roles and expectations made their way into classroom life. Explaining the tension she feels working with boys in class, Bin Qing related this story:

Boys are not better than girls, and girls are not better than boys. One time, I were with some boys, and they said, they say in Chinese, they say, "Boys are better than girls, and girls should, should be [do] all of the housework." And they said, "Boys run out work a lot, and when boys come back, the girls should have dinner for ready for them."

After this story, some other girls brought up explanations for this point of view. One student, named Jenny, mentioned succinctly, "And most . . . I think that is the history of China."

Choosing to ignore that girls come to school even in sixth grade with such a strong sense of gender roles would be choosing to neglect a large part of who my students are. But to what extent and in what ways is it appropriate (or imperative) for me as a teacher to provide alternate possibilities to my students? As much as we may wish to identify with girls, to help them discover their own identity, this discovery cannot come about by treating girls as though they embody a particular culture. As Jenny and Bin Qing's discussion demonstrated, adolescent girls who are immigrants are poised strangely between childhood and adulthood, between China and Chinatown. They try to understand their complex position at a time that, as Carol Gilligan (1993) says, is "indelibly political":

Women teaching girls, then, are faced with a series of intricate problems of relationship. Girls must learn the traditions that frame and structure the world they are entering, and they also must hold on to their own way of hearing and seeing. How can women stay with girls and also teach cultural traditions? How can girls stay with women and also with themselves? What can women teach girls about living in a world that is still governed by men? (pp. 164–165)

Rather than starting from the perspective of changing everything about how girls see themselves in a new country, I wonder how I can start from the classroom. What are the implications for a middle school science classroom of what teachers learn about their students?

The culture of Chinatown is mirrored in the culture of the classrooms in Chinatown. Students bring their biases and habits of speech, their preconceived notions of the roles of teacher and student. Power among students plays out in strange ways. One girl tried to explain why she thinks certain girl students were able to do very well in the class:

I think sometimes, maybe, girls work much more better than boys, and sometimes boys work better than girls. I think one of the reasons girls work much better—maybe they use some of other boys' ideas, to improve that.

Later, another student added:

I think that boys and girls together [in the same class] is better. Because sometimes the girls don't understand the thing that they read, and the boys can help.

These students' comments point to an important realization in my teaching: perhaps girls remain silent not because they are shy (my previous assumption), but because they want to be *right*, to be certain of their ideas *before* saying them. That is, a classroom that privileges students who are quick with an answer may not ever recognize the ideas of students who are less sure of themselves. Unfortunately, as comments like this from different students allowed me to see, this mentality created an odd dynamic in the classroom: boys would shout out their thoughts quickly, even when discouraged to do so, and girls would quietly write these words down and modify them. We faced a strange hierarchy in which boys produced the ideas and girls accepted them.

One way to subvert such a problematic classroom situation in science is to take emphasis away from the idea of "concepts." As soon as classroom learning is based on what Eleanor Duckworth (1996) calls "stated nouns, which one 'has' or 'hasn't'" (p. 53), the teacher allows for those who "have" things more easily to control the classroom. This way of thinking privileges the voice of certain students—those who are taught again and again in life outside school that their words are always most important. I have seen in my ESL classes that this often translates into the silencing of girls as their experiences in school reinforce the notion that boys' ideas are more correct or important. Moreover, if the teacher is doing nothing more than filling students with her preconceived science sequence—what Freire calls the "banking notion"—then students will never learn to question the validity or neutrality of the subject matter (Freire 1970, p. 57).

Instead, I try to encourage all students' individual ideas and to help students see science as questions and problems that have many solutions and that build on a base of knowledge and experience to which we all have access. When I allow students to consult with others instead of rushing the class and demanding an answer, I find more girls willing to speak up. Danling Fu (1995) writes of the silence of many Asian students:

In the Chinese culture we tell our children, "You shouldn't speak up if you are not a hundred percent sure of what you are going to say." So we are always careful of what we say, because we are very conscious of our image to others. (p. 198)

The opportunity to check with others or even to write words down before saying them to the class can really make the difference for girls who are concerned with getting the answer right—especially when the concern about science content is compounded by fear of making mistakes in English.

Allowing students to speak in small groups or talk to each other also allows the needed time to find the English words that are sometimes hard to come by, as in this conversation between two students and me, in which we were talking about ways Chinese schools differ from American schools.

XIAO YU: [The teacher] will want you to . . . to . . . [says a word in Chinese]

JENNY: To remember it.

XIAO YU: Remember. And then, and tomorrow, and when you come in next time . . . want to . . .

JENNY: I know what she means. Want to remember it when you . . . when you read it to someone and you won't need the book, be . . . only because you only need to say it without the book.

KIRAN: Oh! "Memorize!"

As children learning English, Jenny and Xiao Yu are experts at circumlocution: they know how to talk around and around a word until they get the idea across to another person. This is a fabulous skill for studying science, as students try to find the words to explain and describe phenomena they understand. Nonetheless, it demands the time and patience to hear a student out, to try to get to the bottom of her ideas and help her express them in English.

My hope is that a shift in the ways girls are allowed and encouraged to voice their ideas in school will allow them to imagine themselves as English speakers and help them to make confident decisions about their futures. Not yet in high school, middle school-age immigrants are said to be well-poised to learn a new language and go on to succeed in many ways in high school (Scarcella 1990, pp. 29–32). Theoretically, they have a firm grounding in their native language and culture, but they are still young enough to learn English and succeed in American high schools. We must be willing, however, to look at things many different ways, without accepting what the school culture says "all" ESL students need. We must find tactics and approaches that integrate a constant inquiry into the lives and abilities of girls, rather than allowing silence to be an excuse for dismissing their voices. We must find ways to help them believe in their ideas and their wonderfully unique identity as girls, immigrants, scientists, and whatever else they wish to be.

References

Butler, Judith. 1990. *Gender Trouble: Feminism and the Subversion of Identity.* New York: Routledge.

Duckworth, Eleanor. 1996. *The Having of Wonderful Ideas and Other Essays on Teaching and Learning.* New York: Teachers College Press.

Freire, Paulo. 1970. *Pedagogy of the Oppressed.* New York: Continuum.

Fu, Danling. 1995. *"My Trouble Is My English": Asian Students and the American Dream.* Portsmouth, NH: Heinemann.

Gilligan, Carol. 1993. Joining the Resistance: Psychology, Politics, Girls, and Women. In Lois Weis and Michelle Fine, eds., *Beyond Silenced Voices: Class, Race, and Gender in United States Schools.* Albany, NY: State University of New York.

Scarcella, Robin. 1990. *Teaching Language Minority Students in the Multicultural Classroom.* Englewood Cliffs, NJ: Prentice Hall.

Help Me Syndrome

Hasina Deary

It's a typical cartoon scene: Popeye off sailing or toting a sledge hammer doing whatever Popeye does to make a living, while Olive Oyl who does not have a job lounges around. Olive is skinny to the point of hospitalization. Popeye obviously does not share his spinach. Olive Oyl, in her frail condition has a tendency to be vulnerable to Bluto's frequent abductions. Bluto is the big, brawny bully who Popeye grapples with from cartoon to cartoon. Poor Olive is whisked away by the hair or thrown kicking and screaming over Bluto's shoulder. Her only salvation is knowing that Popeye will be coming to save her. "Help me, help me, Popeye!" Magically, he hears Olive's call for help. Popeye, her hero. He struggles with his can of spinach, but in the end the tattooed avenger saves Olive Oyl. It is so silly. Olive Oyl the helpless's only redeeming quality as a woman is the fact she is never stuck in the kitchen. Popeye, the strong and courageous, also prepares his own meals.

Why wasn't Olive ever smart enough to lock the doors so Bluto couldn't get in or clever enough to save herself? It is a disgusting example of the "Help Me Syndrome" so often portrayed in cartoons.

In *Sleeping Beauty,* the silly little princess pricked her finger causing an entire kingdom to slumber. Peace was restored after the prince rode into town, fought with a witch in dragon's form, then kissed the Sleeping Beauty. All is well, another princess saved.

I asked the question: Why are women constantly in need of male rescue? Does the industry feed on some women's twisted fantasy to be saved by a make-believe Prince Charming? It might be said that these are old cartoons and women today have evolved. But I argue that Disney's three latest productions have at least one scene where the female character's life was in jeopardy, only to be spared by her male counterpart

In *The Little Mermaid*, Eric steers a ship's mast through the evil Ursula's torso, freeing Ariel from the curse. After Belle from *Beauty and the Beast* tries to leave the castle she is attacked by slanty-eyed wolves. Lucky for her, the Beast came and fought off the angry hounds. A sigh of relief is breathed, another pretty face saved. Even in *Aladdin*, Disney's most progressive cartoon, Aladdin, the street-smart hero, first comes to Princess Jasmine's aid when she nearly has her hand cut off after being accused of thievery. In the end of the movie, we see Jasmine trapped in a huge hourglass. Her cries for help are drowned out by the sand that fills the glass. Finally, Aladdin breaks the glass to save Jasmine. Ahh.

While the women in Disney's three recent cartoons are a step up from the nonstop pathetic whining of Olive Oyl, they still lack independence and basic survival skills. They may be called a heroine, but by no means are they the woman hero. Indeed, they are merely girls in need of rescue. The misconception that females must be male-dependent is reiterated, even if they basically have things going for them. Belle wanted more than her "provincial life." So they want more, but never can they attain it by themselves.

Rarely do we see brave women saving others. Wonder Woman is the only woman cartoon character I know who has ever been the rescuer. She saves men, women, and children (but mostly women and children). Of course, she has to have Super Heroine powers to do it. She could not just be Mindy MacGyver, the normal girl, who uses her mind to solve problems. Instead cartoons are made about beautiful girls who sing and read, and bright-eyed, headstrong princesses who are all capable of thinking, but ultimately succeed because of the love of a man. I think it is time to change the outdated formulas of love and near-death rescue scenes. I challenge the cartoon makers to find a new happy ending.

10

Arranged Marriages, Rearranged Ideas

Stan Karp

JIHANA WAS one of my favorite students. By the time she was a senior, we had been together for three years, first in a sophomore English class and then through two years of journalism electives where students produced school publications and learned desktop publishing.

Jihana's bright-eyed intelligence and can-do enthusiasm made her a teacher's dream. Her daily greeting in our busy journalism office was, "Hi, Mr. Karp, what needs to be done?" I used to joke that she'd get straight A's until the end of her senior year when I'd have to fail her so she couldn't graduate and leave. It was corny, but she always laughed.

Jihana was one of a growing number of Bengali students in my Paterson, New Jersey, high school. Along with increasing numbers of Latin American, Caribbean, Middle Eastern, Central European, and other immigrants, these new communities had transformed the school in the twenty years I'd been there as a teacher. What had once been a predominantly white, then later, a primarily black and Latino student population, was now thoroughly international.

Increasingly, among my best students each year were young Bengali women. Some, like Jihana, covered their heads with scarves in keeping with Muslim tradition. A few wore the full veil. Others wore no special dress. Many seemed reserved and studious. Others gradually adopted the more assertive, outgoing styles of the citywise teens around them.

By the time Jihana was a senior it was natural to ask, during one of the many extra periods she spent in the journalism office, what her postgraduation plans were. She said she wanted to go to college, perhaps to study medicine, and was considering several schools. But, she added, a lot depended on whether she had to get married.

I knew enough about Jihana, and about the Bengali community, to know that she wasn't referring to a premature wedding prompted by an unplanned pregnancy, but to the possibility of an arranged marriage. Jihana made it pretty clear that she wasn't ready to get married. She was anxious to go to college and to move out of a household where she felt she had too many cleaning chores and child-care duties, and not enough personal freedom. She said the outcome partly depended on what happened with her sister, who was several years older, and also a candidate for marriage, and on whether her family decided to send them both back to Bangladesh in the summer for possible matches.

I listened sympathetically, and made schoolteacher noises about how smart I thought she was and how I hoped she'd get the opportunity to attend college. Unsure of just what my role as a white, male high school teacher could possibly be in this situation, I halfheartedly offered to speak to her family about her college potential if she thought it would help. Jihana smiled politely and said she'd keep me posted.

I went home thinking about Jihana's situation. I was upset, even angered by the thought that this young woman's promising educational future could be sidetracked by a cultural practice that seemed to me hopelessly unreasonable and unfair. The custom of arranged marriages was completely alien to my own sensibilities and to my expectations for my students. I kept thinking of how my own high school-aged daughter, raised at home and, at least nominally, at school, to think in terms of gender equality and independence, would laugh in my face if I ever sat her down and tried to tell her my plans for her marital future.

I also thought, and not for the first time, about what my responsibilities were as a public school teacher; and how I should manage this mix of my own strongly held personal opinions, concern for my students' well-being, and respect for the cultural differences that were increasingly prominent in my school community. I tried to imagine what I could possibly say to her family about the situation: "Hi, I'm Jihana's teacher, and as a politically progressive, pro-feminist, privileged white male, I think your plans for Jihana are a medieval abomination." I don't think so. But the more I thought about it, the more I realized that the problem wasn't finding more diplomatic ways to voice my opinions; the problem was figuring out the dividing line between responding to the needs of my students and interfering inappropriately with "other people's children."

I also thought about another student I had some ten years earlier, Rafia, who faced this same situation. Rafia was the youngest of four daughters in a Bengali family. Smart, sophisticated beyond her years, and ambitious, Rafia was anxious to go to college despite her family's objections. As I encouraged her and helped her fill out applications during her junior and senior years, it was Rafia who first made me aware that many Bengali families did not think girls should go to college, and that she and her sisters were facing, with varying degrees of dread, the prospect of arranged marriages. I was horrified at the idea, and said so. In fact, as I recall, my main reaction consisted in expressing my outrage that women were oppressed this way in her culture. I told her I didn't think anyone had the right to tell her who to marry, and that it was more important for her future to go to college than to please her parents. I even suggested that it was more important to choose college than to avoid a break with her family, and that, even if they got upset, they would probably get over it. I somewhat flippantly told her she could stay at my house for a while if she decided to run away.

When Jihana's story jogged by memory, it was with more than a little embarrassment that I recalled how my reaction to Rafia's had been foolish, and not a little arrogant. I had acted as if the most important response to Rafia's dilemma was to show her that not everyone was so "backward" as her parents, and that there were swell, "enlightened" folks like myself who believed in her right to shape her own future and education. In effect, I was showing off the "superior" values and "advanced" thinking of "progressive western culture," especially of radicals like myself, and contrasting it to the "underdeveloped practices" of her own community, which I encouraged her to reject. I had also reacted as if what I thought and how I felt about the issues raised by her predicament were of paramount importance, and should be the point of departure for my response.

Looking back, it seemed the problem wasn't that I was wrong to make my opposition to the custom of arranged marriages known, but that I did it in a way that was essentially self-serving, and as a practical matter, not very helpful. I had basically denounced what I, as an outsider, saw as "deficient" in her culture and encouraged her to turn her back on it. While my sympathies may have been well-meant, my advice was culturally insensitive and wildly impractical. And it probably just reinforced Rafia's sense of alienation and being trapped.

Fortunately, Rafia was sharp enough to appreciate my personal support and ignore my advice. Instead of running away or openly breaking with her family, she steadfastly argued for her chance to attend college while continuing to excel in school. Eventually, she got her father's permission to go to college (though she was forced to study engineering instead of the humanities she preferred). The experience had stayed with me over the years, and now that a similar situation had arisen, I was anxious to do better by Jihana.

A couple of weeks passed after our first conversation, and it became clear that nothing decisive would happen with Jihana's situation until the summer came. Still looking for a way to lend support, one day I suggested to Jihana that she consider writing a story about arranged marriages for our student magazine. Instead of dwelling on my own opinions, I tried to emphasize that she wasn't the only one facing these issues, and that she could perform a service for both Bengali students and the rest of the school by focusing on a set of concerns that had gotten little attention.

Jihana seemed interested, but hesitant. She was a good writer, but generally took less ambitious assignments like covering school news or activities. She expressed some concern that her family would be offended if they found out, and that, in the tightly knit Bengali community, it might be hard to keep it a secret even if she published a piece anonymously. I asked her to think it over, and told her she could get credit for writing the article even if she decided in the end not to publish it. I also told her, as I did all my students, that we could consider the implications of going public later, but she should write what she really thought and not censor herself in advance. I was hoping to use the tremendous potential that writing has, not only to help students express their ideas and feelings, but also to help them develop the skills, and sometimes the distance, needed to analyze complicated topics and clarify issues. While I hoped Jihana would eventually publish, it seemed valuable to have her organize and express her thoughts for her own purposes as well. After a few days, and after double-checking that she wouldn't have to publish the piece if she wasn't comfortable, she agreed. She asked for help making an outline, so we arranged a story conference.

When we started discussing how to organize the article, Jihana said she wanted to deal first with stereotypes and misconceptions that Westerners had about Muslims. She said she wanted to put the issue of arranged marriages in a broader context of Muslim culture, which had a variety of customs and practices that she felt were misunderstood. Muslim women were not "slaves," she said, and not everyone did things the same way. When it came to marriage, there were a range of practices and, in many cases, Muslim women did have choices and varying degrees of input in the decision.

This led to a discussion of women and marriage customs in general, and how women have faced oppression and male supremacy in all cultures. We also talked about the generational conflict between young Bengalis (and other younger immigrants) raised in the U.S., and their parents, rooted in more traditional, "old country" customs, and how this exacerbated the struggle over marriage practices. Jihana told me stories about families that had been torn apart by these differences, and others where parents and children had found common ground and happy endings.

As we talked, several things became clear. By locating the issue of arranged marriages inside the broader issue of women's rights, which cuts across all cultures and countries, it became easier for Jihana to address the topic without "stigmatizing" her own community. If Bengali women had to wrestle with arranged marriages and male dominance, the supposedly more "liberated" sexual culture of the U.S. presented women with its own set of problems: higher levels of sexual assault, single teenage parenthood, divorce, and domestic violence. Generational conflict between old ways and new also cut across cultures, and made the issue seem more universal, again allowing it to be addressed in a context that didn't demonize one particular group.

Finally, it was clear that speaking on behalf of Bengali women, instead of just against the practice of arranged marriages, tended to make Jihana feel more empowered than isolated. She was still determined to question the imposition of marital arrangements against the woman's will, but would do so in the context of defending Muslim culture against stereotypes and as part of a critique of women's oppression as a whole. Added to the protection she felt from not having to publish her work if she chose not to, assuming this positive stance on behalf of herself and her peers seemed to give her the safe space she needed from which to address these difficult issues. By the end of our conversation, she seemed ready to go. Within a week or two, Jihana was back with her article.

"Do Muslim women have any rights?" she began. "Do they make their own decisions? Are they allowed to think? Are they prisoners in their own homes? There are many stereotypes held by Westerners about the position and role of Muslim women. . . . These notions are based upon the lack of knowledge Westerners have of Islam."

She continued, "Women, regardless of their culture or society, have suffered tremendously over inequality and have had to fight for a firm place in their society. During the Roman civilization, a woman was considered to be a slave. The Greeks bought and sold their women as merchandise rather than accept them as human beings. Early Christianity regarded their women as 'temptresses,' responsible for the fall of Adam.

"In pre-Islamic times, as well as in certain places today, a female child is thought of as a cause for unhappiness and grief. Baby girls were sometimes buried alive after birth. But gaps in wealth, education, and justice between men and women can be found everywhere and just can't be explained by religion."

Jihana went on to discuss "some issues about the rights of a Muslim woman [that] stem from the issue of marriage." She wrote about the varying degrees of choice women may have in different families, the generational conflict, the problems associated with patterns of marriage in the U.S. ("Some Muslim families say that while the Westerners seem to be 'more free,' their society is not working too well.") She cited examples to show that, "As in all marriages, whether arranged or not, some work and some do not."

After exploring the issues from several sides, Jihana came to a balancing act that suggested her own personal struggle. "Arranged marriages, and other Muslim customs of life, like the covering of the body and not dating, may seem to be burdensome to women of most western cultures, but for Muslim women it's their way of life. We were brought up to follow and believe that these practices were the right ways of life. It is up to us as individuals to see that we follow what is expected of us. . . . The Muslim religion, in my opinion, can include double standards. . . . In many cases males are allowed to do certain things that females can't. . . . For example, when a male does get married without his parents' permission, it is okay, but if a female does the same thing it is not okay. This is so because in the Holy Koran it states that a woman has to follow certain things. For example, it is a woman's duty and obligation to bring up her children according to the ways of Islam. She has to look after the family and has absolute control over domestic affairs. She must wear a covering cloak when meeting adult men outside her family. She is her husband's helpmate. Islam recognizes the leadership of a man over a woman, but that does not mean domination.

"In conclusion women should have the freedom and right to do something they're interested in doing or accomplishing. They should go forward with their education if they want to continue it, with the help and support to do so. Women can cook and clean, but they could also do more."

At bottom, Jihana's "balancing" act was an affirmative statement about her place and her rights in her community. And though writing the article didn't resolve her dilemma, it did, I think, support her in her efforts to speak up for herself, and offered a way for her to develop some useful perspectives on her situation. It also helped focus attention on issues that she and her Bengali peers were wrestling with inside the school community.

Though Jihana had originally balked at the idea of publication, by the time she was done she used the computer skills she'd learned in class to create a two-page layout for our magazine with her article, her byline, and her picture under the title "Muslim Women: Where Do We Belong?" She seemed proud of it, and so was I, especially as I reflected on what I'd learned myself.

Switching the focus from my own reactions to my student's point of view, and developing a deeper appreciation of the need to deal with issues of cultural difference with more humility and care, had led me to a more effective and more appropriate response. I was still just as opposed as ever to arranged marriages, and still saw pitfalls and contradictions in Jihana's balancing act about the codes of Islam.

But, because I hadn't begun with an attack on the cultural norms of her community, I had managed to find a way that, to some degree at least, both supported and empowered her.

As it turned out, Jihana's willingness to raise such issues was not limited to our magazine. One morning in the spring, I found her working feverishly in the journalism office on a list of "Bengali Concerns" for the next student government meeting. The list had a tone familiar from earlier days of student activism, but it had specifics I'd never seen before:

1. How come there aren't more Bengali SGA members?
2. There is a lack of Bengali students involved in school activities. We need more participation and more representation of the Bengali people.
3. We need Bengali-speaking guidance counselors and teachers.
4. We need Bengali mentors.
5. How come the history teachers never teach about Bangladesh and its culture when they teach world history?
6. Why isn't there Bengali student representation when the school presents a panel of students to represent the school?
7. How come all the newsletters that go home from the school are either in Spanish or in English? How come you can't send letters home that are in Bengali? That way the parents will know what is going on in their children's school. The lack of communication with the Bengali parents is a reason why many don't attend the home-school council meetings.

Around the same time that these concerns were being presented to the student government, preparations were under way for an assembly presentation of Bengali dance and traditional dress. Like many other schools, my high school is still in the relatively superficial stages of addressing multicultural issues, and tends toward food festivals and holiday celebrations. But the assembly program tapped the energy of many Bengali students, and Jihana had gotten involved. One afternoon, soon after our magazine had appeared, she came to the journalism office and asked if I could fax a copy of her article to a reporter from a local newspaper. She'd said she'd been interviewed in connection with the upcoming assembly program, but had left some things out. "I was trying to explain myself to the reporter and couldn't get the words out right," she said. "I told him I had written an article explaining what I thought, and it was all in there. I promised to send it to him." The article she had been hesitant to write and reluctant to publish had become a personal position statement.

As we headed into the last weeks of the school year, I occasionally asked Jihana if there were any new developments. There weren't any on the marriage front, but she did get accepted to several colleges, and began to make plans to attend a state university. When we parted at year's end, I made her promise to let me know how things turned out.

About a month later, I returned from a trip to find a slightly ambiguous message. Jihana had called, to say hello and to invite me to a wedding. Taken aback, and fearing that this might be her way of letting me know that marriage had won out over college, I called her at home. She was in good spirits and busy getting ready to move into the dorms on her new campus. The invitation was to her sister's wedding, Jihana explained, and if I could come I'd get a chance to see some more of how Bengali marriage customs worked. Unfortunately, I wasn't able to attend, but Jihana promised to show me the proceedings on videotape.

In September Jihana started college classes. A few weeks later, I got a note describing her new life. "College is okay," she wrote, "not that great as everyone said it would be. Maybe it is just me. I never realized how difficult my classes would be and so large in lectures!! I am taking an Arabic class so that I can be trilingual!

"I have to go home every weekend, but I don't mind. I have a new status in my family; everyone respects me more, and I also don't have to do any more housework. Isn't that great??!!" I had to agree that it was.

The Wrath of Guess Jeans

Jessica Zarins

Walking down the halls of Sellwood Middle School was like encountering a ravenous beast, ready to gobble you up. Between the snobby rich Eastmoreland girls and the overly preppy Eastmoreland jocks, I was immediately stamped with the words "fashion reject" from day one. My two-year-old white and purple Pro-Wings were falling apart and my grungy Levis weren't cutting it anymore, either. Everyone was suddenly wearing Guess jeans. "Guess?" I thought, "Guess what?" I felt like the only person in the world who didn't understand the concept of Guess jeans but I certainly understood the importance of them and how they were absolutely *essential* at Sellwood.

I had been talking about Guess jeans for weeks before my mom actually took me to Meier & Frank to take a look at them. When we got to the juniors section and found the Guess jeans my mom almost had a heart attack. "Sixty dollars!" she gasped, as she peered at the price tag. "I'm sorry, honey, but I really can't afford these."

As I watched her put the jeans back on the rack, I felt like I had had my heart ripped out of my chest and thrown into a pit of wild bears. After all the talk of how important these jeans were to me, they were too expensive? I wasn't having it. The whining began.

"But Mooooooom! All the girls have them and they won't let me hang with them if I don't have them. I'll be the only girl without . . ." I pleaded, pulling on her shirt sleeve. My whining immediately got cut short when she said in what sounded to me like a yell, "*WELL, I GUESS WE COULD GO TO VALUE VILLAGE AND TRY TO FIND A PAIR THERE!*"

Looking around desperately to see if anyone had heard, I hoped I wouldn't see anyone I knew or might *ever* know. I moved quickly to look through clothes about two racks away so no one would think I was with my mom, the person who had literally yelled out the dread words, "Value Village."

Value Village? How could my mom have said that in front of everyone at Meier & Frank? I was appalled. Obviously she understood nothing and did not care about me or how I felt. Value Village was the place the popular kids ridiculed and degraded. They yelled at kids in the halls with the insult, "You buy your clothes at Value Village!'' They said it was a place for homeless people and welfare recipients. After we were back in the car, I decided that if Guess jeans might be there I would have to take my chances.

We drove off in our '67 blue Chevy, otherwise known as the Blue Bomber—the same car I made my mom park behind a trailer two blocks away from my school so the popular kids wouldn't see me—and in no time we were in the Value Village parking lot.

Entering Value Village, the stench of disinfectant lingered in the air, assaulting my nose with every breath. Struggling to hold my breath, I walked toward the jeans rack where I immediately spotted Carmen, one of the popular girls at Sellwood. She saw me, turned beet red, and ran down the aisle and out the door. I was so astounded that one of the popular girls was at Value Village, I almost forgot my purpose. But then, remembering why I was there, I promptly looked for and found a pair of Guess jeans, slightly frayed at the ends, purchased them, and went home.

The next day at school, wearing my most fashionable Guess jeans and dressing down at the girls' locker room, I heard snickering behind me. I turned around and found all the popular girls in a clump, pointing, laughing, and whispering.

Rebecca, the leader of the pack, who could be clearly identified by her pearly pink lip gloss and her six-inch bangs, which always reeked of Aqua Net, suddenly piped up, ''Nice jeans, Jessica. Was Value Village having a half-price sale?''

''Yeah, too bad you can't afford the real thing!'' mimicked Carmen, both hands placed defiantly on her hips.

I was completely mortified. After all my hard work to finally fit in, my prized possession Guess jeans weren't even considered ''the real thing'' because they came from Value Village. It was then I realized that the popular girls were obviously never going to be my friends because they were rich, preppy snobs and I didn't need them to criticize me anyway. From that day on, I never wanted to be popular again.

11

The Lowdown on Life, Sex, and Your Bod: Learning from Girls' Unofficial Literacy

Ruth Shagoury Hubbard

AMY LEANED across the double desks, and giggling, broke off a corner of Tara's granola bar. Tara playfully slapped her friend's hand: "Oo, your nail polish looks cool! I'm gonna try two colors tonight, too!" She popped the rest of the bar into her own mouth, and crumpled the wrapper. Around her, the other seventh-grade students were finishing their snacks, returning to their desks, and shuffling through papers.

As Mrs. Baxter gave the directions for the social studies groups' assignments, Tara tore a page out of her loose-leaf notebook, and jotted a note to her friend: "Dear Amy, Sorry I kept bugging you about who you like. Do you really like Travis? If you do, that's okay. Going to the mall sounds cool. Maybe Thursday or Friday since we both don't have school. That would be a ton of fun! You made me feel better when you told me about Corinna. Thanks. Well, I need to go now! BuBye, Tara. P.S. I hope I'll see you on Thursday or Friday!"

After precisely folding the note into a diamond shape, Tara penciled "Amy" in a careful cursive, then casually dropped the message on her friend's desk as she walked by on her way to meet with her social studies group.

GIRLS IN early adolescence are at a particularly vulnerable time, creating or re-creating their identities as they form their perceptions of themselves and their social world, including expectations for the future. Literacy plays a key role in regulating adolescent girls' subculture; girls like Amy and Tara use literacy as an important part of their social process. When these adolescent girls write, what is the cultural context that surrounds their literacy?

Studies of writing typically focus on the "official" writing that students create during the course of the school day. But as educational ethnographers begin to look at the broader context surrounding students' writing, another layer is being uncovered. In her detailed ethnography of an urban junior high school, Amy Shuman (1986) discusses the use of writing as play for adolescents, including categories such as adult forms of writing for adolescent purposes, and parodies of adult genres students choose to do on their own. Margaret Finders's (1997) recent study explores the role of a range of literacy events in middle school girls' lives—events such as signing yearbooks, writing notes and bathroom graffiti, reading "teen 'zines" and doing homework together.

Intrigued by references to these "unofficial" contexts for writing, I wondered what I could learn about the forces that are shaping adolescent girls by examining the ways they use writing and reading for their own purposes. What values keep these forms of literacy going? How are they affecting the ways they make sense of themselves as individuals—and present themselves as they move into adulthood?

Context for the Study

I DECIDED to turn to native informants to learn more about their literacy events. Over the course of a year as resident researcher in a sixth-grade classroom, children like Amy and Tara taught me the recipes for behavior in their complex social world, sharing their reading and writing with me and explaining the rites and rituals that are a part of the cultural context of their literacy. Building on this research base, I have spent the last six months conducting interviews with girls in grades six through eight at four other research sites. (The five research sites represent rural, urban, and suburban communities at a range of socioeconomic levels.)

These middle school girls collected and saved the notes they write to each other, telling me about how and why they write them, relaying stories that surround the notes themselves, and also showing me the magazines they like to read and the ways they share them with each other. I met with the girls both individually and in groups of two and three, tape-recording the interviews and, with their permission, photocopying the notes they talked about and read to me. Finally, I shared the emerging findings with a group of older adolescents in order to see if the patterns I was noting would ring true to them. They not only confirmed these findings by their recollections from their recent past, they have been instrumental in creating "action plans" to address the needs of middle school students.

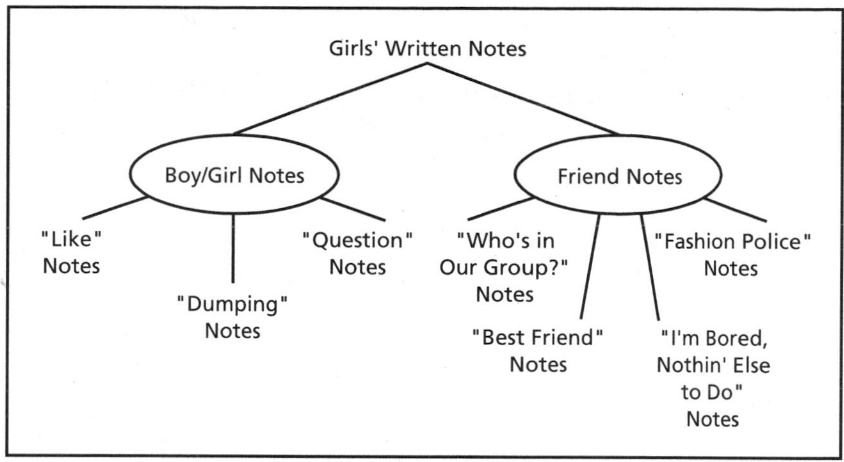

Figure 11.1 Categories of girls' written notes.

Categories of Written Notes

WRITTEN NOTES are an important component of the daily lives of the sixth-, seventh-, and eighth-grade girls I observed and interviewed. Together, we looked through literally hundreds of notes; some were hilarious, others heartbreaking, and many were poignant reminders of the world of adolescence. It was the girls themselves who created categories in the kinds of notes they wrote. I believe it's important to understand the boundaries *they* have formed around the different uses of literacy rather than relying on my own adult lenses for ordering the data (see Figure 11.1).

Boy/Girl Notes

At each school, the girls created a similar category that they ranked as the most important kind of note they send and receive. These could be termed "Like" Notes. Anyone who has recently worked in a middle school or junior high won't be surprised to hear that the most common conversation starter and message lead is: "Who do you like?" Tara's note to Amy, quoted at the beginning of the chapter, begins with a reference to earlier "like" notes when she writes, "Sorry to keep bugging you about who you like. Do you really like Travis?" Sometimes, choices are offered:

MARK:

Do you like

Donna	or	Christine
yes	both	yes
no		no

Please answer!

It's important to these sixth, seventh, and eighth graders to see their relationships in print; it appears to give them more reality, and sometimes permanency, although the shifting relationships are quite difficult to keep up with. This preoccupation with pairing up into boy/girl relationships seems to be more a play ritual than really "dating" in the same way as older adolescents do. Instead, these younger girls and boys appear to be acting out what they see as their future roles. "Going with" someone in middle school lingo usually means that you are seen as a couple by the school community, and perhaps talk on the telephone a few times a week. It doesn't mean that the couple actually "goes out" anywhere together.

Another category that deals with these ever-changing boy/girl relationships was identified for me by Shannon, when she offered to read a letter to me that she called a "Dumping" Note:

[Excerpt from transcript, October 22, 1997]

SHANNON: [reading] I'm sorry but I'm afraid I'm not happy with this relationship. I'm sure you will go on to find a better guy for yourself. I have to break up with you because our relationship is too imbalanced. We are like oil and water. We will never fully mix. It was great while it lasted though I hope that you aren't too hurt. I'm terribly sorry that this has to happen like this, but we are as different as night and day. I just can't work up the guts to tell you this in person because I know I will break down and you will try to convince me out of this again. We both know it will never work

between us and it will only stab us more if we continue this relationship. I'm so sorry that I have to do this.
Love, Daniel
P.S. There is no other girl.

RUTH: And he really did write this?

SHANNON: No!

RUTH: No?

GIRLS: No! Lori did—he had Lori write it, 'cause he wouldn't.

RUTH: But he meant it. I mean, he wanted her to get this information. It's not like a fake note or something? But somebody else wrote it.

SHANNON: Right.

AMY: He's been about to dump her a lot . . . because . . .

STEPHANIE: Yeah, 'cause he doesn't want to do it, 'cause . . . [her voice trails off]

RUTH: Okay, so tell me more about this note. So how did you happen to get this note? Since it's not to you . . .

SHANNON: Because, I'm the deliverer.

AMY: Yeah, the deliverer.

RUTH: So, you're the deliverer. So has she gotten this note yet?

STEPHANIE: No.

SHANNON: No!

STEPHANIE: She's not going to. She's in A Hall.

SHANNON: I have to wait for Daniel to give me the word and he's just afraid.

RUTH: Oh, my gosh . . .

AMY: Yeah, Daniel doesn't want her to get it 'cause then, 'cause she's in A Hall, and we're at lunch when she's outside at gym, so today, he wanted me to go with him when he dumped her and stuff.

There is a great deal going on in this exchange. It was clear from the excitement in the girls' voices that this was the drama—or trauma—of the day. Shannon has the high-status position of "deliverer" of the note, which appeared to be the ritual at this school when someone is "dumped" by a member of the opposite sex. As deliverer, Shannon has both knowledge and power; because she is privy to the information in the note, she can decide with whom to share that knowledge. In this case, she shares it eagerly with her group, showing her allegiance to them, and with me, indicating her high status in that she is frequently chosen to convey and deliver messages from boys. She is still "waiting for the word," though, from Daniel, and at the point she read this note to me on tape, Sonja, the girl it was written to, had not yet received it! Clearly, she has the lowest status in this encounter, and no empathy from this circle of girls; after all, their classes are in C Hall, while Sonja's are in A Hall (rival territory).

Amy makes sure we all know that she, too, has a role in this drama: Daniel wants her at his side when he watches Shannon deliver the note. In this incident, though Daniel is at the center, almost every aspect of the literacy event has been orchestrated by the girls, from Lori helping him craft the note, to Shannon delivering it, to Amy standing by at his side. This was part of a clear pattern I noted at each school: though the boys were very rarely the initiators in note writing, any involvement on the part of the boys was highly prized. For example, though only 20 percent of the notes in the pile Shannon, Amy, and Stephanie shared with me were written by boys, those were the ones they showed me exclusively at first, stressing that these would be the best ones for me to copy.

Each of these girls showed me copies of notes written to them by boys from a category they named "Question" Notes. These notes were the most prized of all, as they *were* initiated by the boys. Though the "question" is seldom explicitly asked, it's not hard to tell what it refers to, as this note shows:

Dear Stephanie:

Well . . . I am really really curious to what my answer is. I can understand if you say no. I mean, I am still going to be your friend, always and forever.

Now I'll get off that. Brendan likes Shannon. He made me look like a fool. I mean he said last Friday. I don't like Shannon . . . and he won't admit it. Oh, well, I'm going to get him to ask her out.

Let me help you with your answer, if you don't write me or pull me to the side, I'll know the answers no. By the end of today.

Always, Micah

The high status of these notes is easily confirmed, not only by the pride with which the girls share them, but the flurry of follow-up notes that surround the event of receiving one of them.

A preoccupation with the boys, their attitudes toward girls, and even their ranking was made clear to me through another key literacy event in one of the seventh-grade classes: the creation of "The List." A two-page, typed and photocopied list was making the rounds at one of the schools I researched, to the chagrin of the teachers, who suggested I interview The List's creators.

Shawna, Carlin, and Melanie furnished me with a copy of The List they had created, typed, and distributed to each member of their class. The List contained a ranking of boys in each of the following sixteen categories: Cutest, Funniest, Most Athletic, Meanest, Smartest, Coolest, Nicest Hair, Best Dressed, Nicest, Cutest Smile, Best Eyes, Biggest Flirt, Sweetest, Most Annoying, Least Trustworthy, and Most Full of Himself. Clearly, physical appearance is the main indicator for these rankings.

These categories and the rankings of the boys are considered "official" by its creators; after all, they checked with the girls in their extended group and went to the time and effort of formalizing it and distributing it. When I asked if other groups disagreed with their list, they were scornful:

RUTH: But what about the other people? Do they ever write on it and change it?

SHAWNA: Yes!

MELANIE and CARLIN [chiming in]: Yes!

CARLIN: They pretend like it makes a difference.

SHAWNA: They cross out "Cutest" and add someone they like . . .

MELANIE: Yeah, some girls wanted to make another one, because they didn't like that one, but they put different categories on.

CARLIN: 'Cause we have different, like friends, and like, we have a schoolwide group, and . . .

SHAWNA: They have their little A Hall group, that thinks they're sooo cool.

RUTH: Mm-hmm. So, this is really the official one?

CARLIN: Yeah, 'cause we did something with it—'cause we made so many copies.

This exchange again emphasizes the importance of the literacy as creating some sense of permanence. It also points out the boundaries and allegiances among the girls' groups. In fact, it is notes among the girls themselves, often working out their tangled maze of relationships and allegiances, that make up the great majority of the notes they write.

Friend Notes

Some girls? They have these stupid little fights, like, "I'm never going to talk to you again," then 20 minutes later, it's like, "Oh, I forgive you! We're friends forever." But we don't do that 'cause we're not like that. That's like the Stacy/Leslie group. (Shawna, Grade 7)

Though the Boy/Girl Notes may have the higher status, the ups and downs of the girls' relationships with each other are the meat and potatoes of their note writing. It is not by chance that The List was created solely of categories for boys. While the girls had no fears of offending the boys on their list, they were much more aware of the possibilities of hurting their friends' feelings—and the havoc that could wreak. When I asked them specifically if they had considered doing a similar list for the girls in their class, their response was an emphatic "No!" They struggled to articulate why:

CARLIN: That would kinda make us rude.

RUTH: It would?

MELANIE: Yeah, 'cause if you didn't put them . . .

SHAWNA: Guys don't care about that stuff, but girls have feelings. . . . It would hurt. . . .

CARLIN: . . . if your friends didn't think that you were in the Nicest or something like that you'd be like . . . really mad at them. . . .

SHAWNA: It can kinda hurt your feelings. . . . I mean, you like to *think* you know what your friends think of you, but if you really knew sometimes . . .

The main problem with having a "Girls' List," they decided, was that it couldn't be an "honest" list because you'd have to put all the girls in each category so no one's friendships would be affected!

The girls named four categories under the larger umbrella of Friend Notes: "Who's in Our Group" Notes, "Best Friend" Notes, "I'm Bored, Nothin' Else to Do" Notes, and "Fashion Police" Notes. "Who's in Our Group?" Notes are a way to keep track of the shifting boundaries around the girls' groups, and are often an attempt to get back into a group of friends' good graces:

Dear Stephanie,

I am really really sorry about the other day. I walked away because I didn't want to fight with you. Tara and Jenny are giving me a real hard time. They keep saying I don't deserve to be your friend. I want to be. Honest.

Love, Rosa

As this note demonstrates, an argument between two friends causes the other members of the group to take sides. One of the girls I interviewed, Claire, depended largely on e-mail for her note writing, and told me about the added dangers current technology can bring:

Claire: This one person was really mad at me? And I was writing notes on e-mail and saying, "Why are you being so mean?" and this and that, and she forwarded them on to her friend! *And so her friend was against me, too. And so, she did that with every single note I wrote her. And I didn't know it at the time.*[1]

"Best Friend" Notes tend to affirm the closeness of the relationship between two girls, sharing special information or offering support in time of need. There is a real reaching out through the writing—planning together, bonding, and empathizing. In the following note, Kate shows Shelley she understands how she feels, tries to plan activities to take Shelley's mind off her troubles, and ends by reaffirming that she is always there to talk to:

To Shelley:

I'm sorry about John. I think he's letting popularity go to his head. You were the ones that deserved him. I'm not saying that I don't like Jen or anything, but you were the one who should have got him. Anyway, I want you to come over some time this vacation. We could walk to the store and buy presents. Anyway, I have to go.

Love, Kate

P.S. If you need someone to talk to, talk to me.

"I'm Bored, Nothin' Else to Do" Notes have less importance attached to them, but seem to fulfill a need to keep communication going. The girls described these notes as "just something to do when you're bored with class." There are usually references within these notes, though, that cross over into the other categories, hinting at issues of interest, such as who likes who or who's in what group:

Stephanie and Amy:

whz ↑ [what's up?] This story is lame. I could fall asleep now. What is going on over there? Shannon and I have fun over here alone. We write notes to each other. I want you guys and Shannon and I to sit in a group. Do you think Rod still likes you Steph? God. I'm bored. Mr. Clark chooses loser stories. If you guys can, write back.

Jenny and Shannon

One of the most fascinating—and discouraging—categories is the one the girls named "Fashion Police" Notes (see Figure 11.2). When I asked Stephanie about the note, penciled onto a Post-it note, she told me, "Oh, that's about this girl, and she wears the same sweatshirt like every single day."

Figure 11.2 Fashion police note.

"Yeah," Amy added. "So we go, 'Fashion Police! Fashion Police!' "

Short and pointed, these notes stress the boundaries around girls set by clothes, appearance, and very often, social class. And just as the self-described "trendsetters" like Amy and Stephanie look down on girls who "don't know how to dress cool," other girls find following the popular trends an indication of superficiality. Emma, an eighth grader at an urban school, gave me an example of how quickly—and mindlessly—clothes fashions sweep through a school among certain groups of girls:

EMMA: Like, when one person that's really popular in the eighth grade starts wearing something, then lots of other people follow. Like, someone started wearing this really bright yellow coat. And then, I was counting them at lunch, and there was seven yellow coats! And they were the exact same yellow coat!

RUTH: Do you feel that kind of pressure, or not really?

EMMA: No. I just wear what I wear.

For the rest of our conversation, Emma referred to the girls whose wardrobes are dictated by what's in with the popular group as "the yellow coats." Though she doesn't adhere to these trends, Emma confirmed what girls at all the other sites had told me: what girls wear marks them as part of a particular grouping within the school, and that "the yellow coats" rely on particular stores (Gap is the most often cited) and certain teen fashion magazines ("teen 'zines") as their fashion resources. The teen 'zines may be touted as a fashion resource by most young adolescents, but they also serve another role—as dispensers of information of a girl's place in the adolescent world and beyond.

Why Teen 'Zines?

RUTH: I was wondering about what kind of reading you do that's just for fun?

SHANNON: We read lots of magazines.

RUTH: Like what magazines?

SHANNON: *YM, Seventeen* . . .

RUTH: What is it you like about them?

AMY: We could bring some in for you. There's lots of advice, and like . . .

STEPHANIE: . . . and guy stories. . .

SHANNON: And romantic stories, and humor, and stories about yourself, questions and quizzes and stuff.

STEPHANIE: You can send in things—you can ask them things you've been wondering about, but you've been kind of afraid to ask people.

SHANNON: Yeah, like about really personal stuff, like your period or stuff like that.

WRITTEN NOTES appear to be the most important aspect of girls' "unofficial writing"—and when it comes to "unofficial reading," teen 'zines seem to be the material of choice. For this reason, they can open up an important window into what girls are both interested in—and in turn, being socialized into. And they likely reach for the quick advice in these magazines partly because they have *already begun* that socialization process; the 'zines give them a deeper guide into something they've already been given cultural clues about. Girls turn to these monthly magazines to explore the same issues they do in their written notes: (1) to know what to do in different situations, especially in relationships with boys; (2) to know how to dress; (3) to show what group you're in; and (4) to learn more about what it will be like to be a teenager. Or, as Shauna expressed it to me, "to get the lowdown on life, sex, and your bod."

The managing editor of *Seventeen* would agree that this is the theme of the content she supervises; in her words, it is meant "to inform, entertain, and give teen-aged girls all the information they need to make sound choices in their lives" (Pierce 1990, p. 496). But a brief look at the articles, advertisements, language, and visuals in magazines such as *Seventeen, Sassy, Teen, YM,* and *Teen People* (the latest entry as of January 1998) show both a narrow range of topics and a very limited range of choices for females in their lives and in their roles. The emphasis in these magazines is on appearance, makeup and fashion, and boys, boys, boys.

In their interviews with me, they stress the fact that they can read these magazines to find out about "woman-type stuff" without having to turn to the adults around them. They feel the authors in the magazines "get" what it's like to be an adolescent today and can inform them of what to expect in the next few years. They use the articles and features as conversation starters to discuss the issues and questions that are on their mind.

What do the girls turn to first? Overwhelmingly, the quizzes and question-and-answer sections. These features run each month in all the different magazines and provide recipes for how to act in certain situations: "Love Crisis: We Solve Your Boy Probs Pronto"; "The Lowdown on Kissing"; and "Are You a Good Friend?" serve up pat answers for girls seeking answers.

If you take *Seventeen's* quiz, for example, you can "find out how you rate on the bud system" ("Are You a Good Friend?" [Spring] 1997). The items on this quiz actually serve to constrain rather than open up choices, socializing girls into unhealthy roles. The multiple choice quizzes, like much of the rest of the material in the magazine, reinforce passive "solutions," the importance of one standard of appearance (with an emphasis on *thin*), and relationships to boys:

10. *What would you do if your best friend's one-and-only started hitting on you?*
    a.) *Pretend it wasn't happening.*
    b.) *Hit back. He's a real Leo.*
    c.) *Ask him if he knows how to spell "loyalty" and walk away.*

Not only are the choices narrow and superficial, the questions around what it means to be a friend are not defined by the girls themselves. Instead, they are the receivers of an already set agenda, subtly and not-so-subtly socialized into a particular worldview.

Appearance, the girls learn from these magazines, is everything. Even articles such as "Like Yourself as You Are" (*YM*) that might be seen in a positive light as fostering a healthy body and self-image seem hypocritical: if girls are supposed to like themselves as they are, why does the same issue have two features on makeovers?

Advertisements make up the bulk of the magazines; in fact, it's difficult to tell the features and stories from the ads themselves. The makeovers, for instance, offer advice from "Maybelline makeup pro Kat" who (surprise!) suggests all Maybelline products to sculpt a new face for thirteen-year-old Audrey. Unfortunately, when magazine publishers and advertisers look at young girls like Audrey, they don't see a girl at a critical stage of her life, they see a representative of a huge target market to be tapped—and in turn molded to become future consumers.

Exploring Girls' Sense of Themselves—and Their Possible Selves

As adolescent girls move into adulthood, they are creating personas—"presenting" themselves, to borrow sociologist Erving Goffman's metaphor. We each "present" ourselves as we want to be seen (Watson and Potter 1962), announcing the personalities we wish to project, the kinds of responses we invite from others, and the boundaries we have created for ourselves.

Like other educators in this collection, my view of the way various aspects of society socialize young girls into gendered roles has been shaped by the important work of researchers and psychologists such as Carol Gilligan and Mary Pipher. This research base can help make visible what is difficult for us—as members of the same culture that is shaping adolescents—to see. But as important as this work is, I believe we need to expand on it and begin to explore the *lived* experiences of girls. Gilligan's work, for example, is based largely on self-reports, but doesn't look at girls in the midst of their adolescent culture, with the rules and rituals that inform their daily routines. If we are interested in cultural acquisition, we need to conduct research that looks at what individuals learn from their culture, as well as the processes by which they learn it. As Spindler and Spindler remind us, "People do not learn *all* that culture presents to them, and different individuals do not learn in the same way" (1991, p. 275).

The girls I talked to are looking for advice and information about what to expect in the years ahead. One important message that comes across clearly is that they look to older teens to try to figure out what life will be like—what possibilities exist for them. They try on these roles in their note taking and assume that the information in the teen 'zines comes from the older girls they wish to emulate. High school-age students seem a logical group to turn to for advice on helping their younger brothers and sisters. Since they are the main role models for middle school kids, the information they share with their younger audience has a greater impact.

When I shared these data with Linda Christensen's high school class at Jefferson High School (Portland, Oregon), they floored me with their insights and enthusiasm for showing younger kids the wider range of options they really have. Several have eagerly entered into "action plans" to work with middle school students, creating a curriculum that shows them unlimited choices for their emerging identities. Some of these high school students are writing essays about their own experiences a few short years ago, such as the essays that are sprinkled through this collection. Others are creating resources: annotated reading lists or writing guidelines for critiquing information and images in teen 'zines and the media in general. These resources fill a gaping hole in needed resources for young adolescents.

And there is a genuine role for adults in our girls' lives, too. Women like Maureen Barbieri and Kiran Purohit (see Chapters 4 and 9) are creating those "pockets of time" to get to know what is going on in their girls' minds, forging strong, genuine connections and support. Evidence is mounting for the dangers of relying on outdated developmental theories that falsely assume that adolescence is naturally a period of separation and alienation from adults. Margaret Finders, in her landmark book *Just Girls,* provides a fascinating and well-documented synthesis of this research and concludes that "we should acknowledge and nurture the connectedness that adolescents feel to adults" (1997, p. 122).

Through really listening to them, we can discover a more genuine understanding of girls at this age—their needs, what they're looking for, and how their friends, popular culture, the school community, and the adults in their lives are filling those needs. We can also examine the ways that their literacy—and their identities—are being shaped by the wider culture's construction of gender roles. It's important to remember that the socialization process for girls is not set in stone, nor does it affect each girl in an identical manner. If people who care about adolescents can learn more information like this, we can create action plans to build on positive aspects and counter the more destructive forces. As we uncover the processes at work as different individuals make sense of themselves, we can learn better ways to explore imaginative strategies to help them accomplish a wider array of hopes and dreams. Then, girls will be able to imagine different perceptions of themselves—and their own possibilities.

Endnote

1 Interviews with girls like Claire who use electronic mail, chat rooms, "Buddy Chats," and other forms of telecommunications uncovered fascinating patterns in their unofficial literacy. A detailed discussion is beyond the scope of this chapter. Perhaps the most

interesting overall finding is that the basic categories remain the same despite the change in medium.

References

Finders, Margaret. 1997. *Just Girls: Hidden Literacies and Life in Junior High*. Urbana, IL: National Council of Teachers of English.

Pierce, Kate. 1990. A Feminist Theoretical Perspective on the Socialization of Teenage Girls Through *Seventeen* Magazine. *Sex Roles* 23, 9/10: 491–500.

Shuman, Amy. 1986. *Storytelling Rights: The Uses of Oral and Written Texts by Urban Adolescents*. New York: Cambridge University Press.

Spindler, George, and Louise Spindler. 1991. Reactions and Worries. *Anthropology and Education Quarterly* 22: 274–278.

Watson, Jean, and Robert Potter. 1962. An Analytic Unit for the Study of Interaction. *Human Relations* 15, 3: 245–263.

12

Traveling Through the Darkness: Allison's Awakening

Stephen A. Brand

. . . For it is important that awake people be awake, or a breaking line may discourage them back to sleep; the signals we give—yes or no, or maybe—should be clear: the darkness around us is deep.

WILLIAM STAFFORD, *A Ritual to Read to Each Other*

I NOTICED Allison the first day of class. She walked in the door, head down, no backpack or books in her hands, and found a seat in the farthest corner of my mentor's classroom. With her oversized denim jacket as a pillow, she slumped at her table and buried her head. From the edge of the class, I looked through the swirl of incoming students. Most walked into the room in pairs or in larger groups and sized up spaces close to their friends. But Allison sat alone. Silence attracts my attention, and this young woman's quiet pierced the chatter of the classroom.

Allison reminded me of the young girls I worked with as a mental health therapist. During the first few weeks, she camouflaged herself in the chaotic landscape of school. She missed days at a time and rarely turned in her work. My mentor and I both worried about Allison's possible substance abuse; her eyes often appeared vacant and remote. When drugs or parties were mentioned in class, she usually snickered in that adolescent manner that says, "Yeah, I know what you're talking about." But it seemed like a nervous laugh, as if she knew she may be headed down a dangerous road.

Allison met Kevin in this class. They walked together and sat with each other during lunch. Like Allison, Kevin seemed more at ease sitting quietly. His large size belied a gentle nature, not unnoticed by the obviously vulnerable Allison. Three months into school, the car Kevin was driving, with Allison in the front seat and two other students in the back, rolled. Kevin was crushed; he died, while Allison and the others survived with minor injuries. Kevin's height may have saved the lives of his friends; it made me wonder how to treat a topic such as tragic irony sensitively when kids live it so starkly.

When I took over the American Literature class one month after the accident, we began reading the novel *Of Mice and Men*. The story inspired intense discussions among the students. I was encouraged to see the young women in the class speak forcefully as issues of gender roles and sex bias surfaced from our reading. Curly's wife, "the tart," became a touchstone for dialogue.

But Allison withdrew even more after the accident. One day she slipped me a note. It read:

Mr. Brand, please don't call on me unless my hand is raised. I'm really nervous to speak in front of people. At Kevin's funeral, I spoke to the entire crowd. Now I can't even speak out anymore. I'll raise my hand if I want to talk.

Thank you.

I promised not to call on her until she was ready. She never said a word during discussions and never asked questions, but she would respond to my greeting each day she attended class. When I asked about her attendance, she spoke about work and the difficulties at home. She said she liked the class and always promised to attend more regularly. However, she continued to miss class at an alarming rate. Allison's attendance records confirmed a pattern of absences in her other classes as well.

At one point she admitted she was thinking about dropping out of school. A primary concern for teachers and others involved in adolescent development—parents, administrators, religious leaders, counselors—is to keep kids in school. Enough evidence exists about the positive effects of school on at-risk children to support extraordinary measures and extraordinary effort to keep adolescents involved in a school structure. The alternative is bleak for most adolescents who drop out of school. In Allison's case, with her apparent home discord, probable substance abuse, and dearth of support outside of school, dropping out would be disastrous.

Two months into my student teaching, I walked down the hall to make transparencies. The day before, we had read parts of Thoreau's writings out loud, and students focused on the conflict between preserving land and developing land. Many students voiced strong opposition to the unabated growth of their town. However, students from the recently developed areas argued that people who work hard enough have a right to reward themselves and live anywhere they want. The discussion escalated and many students walked to the next class disturbed by the varying points of view.

I had created the transparencies to show students optical illusions, like the well-known drawing that depicts an old hag or a glamorous young woman, depending on how you look at it. I was hoping to inspire a discussion that would validate multiple viewpoints and allow students an opportunity to explore how they create their perceptions. I knew the students would look at the same pictures but see different images, much like their different views of the city and its development.

On my way down the hall, I noticed a group of students, three boys and two girls, sitting on the floor. School had yet to start, and as I walked by, one boy looked at me, nodded, and said, "What's up?" I had never seen this boy before, or anyone else in the group. I heard their laughter as I walked past.

In groups, adolescents seem to share a secret they teasingly dangle in front of adults, as if to say, "We know something you don't know, and we'll never tell." The secret often seems personal against anyone outside their circle and carries an intimidating tone with the stares, silence, and laughter. I felt that ridicule.

As soon as I turned the corner, one of the boys shouted at someone I hadn't seen walking down the hall the other way. In mock question, he asked his friends, "She's a dyke right? She's a lesbo?" I heard chuckles from his friends, then, "Yeah, she's a dyke. She's definitely a dyke."

I turned the corner, away from the students, and leaned against the wall, almost out of breath from what I had heard. I was stunned not only at the words themselves but at the ease at which they slipped from the mouth of this young man. The language fit perfectly in a familiar phrase, practiced like poetry or lines in a play, and the speaker's comfort in the words echoed down the hall and in my head. No reply came from the target of their attack and silence filled the hall.

I stood around the corner and leaned against the wall. I did nothing. Dialogue began to race through my head. I thought about my peers and our discussions of diversity and community and safety. Throughout the year, my peers and I had challenged each other to create safe environments for students, but private talk in small groups is different than public action. I was now a public school teacher and, like teachers I had self-righteously ridiculed, I stood passively by.

The silence served as a vacuum as I withdrew into myself and thoughts began to swirl. The previous week my classmates and I had listened to six young men and women from the group Roots and Branches describe their experience in high school. Gay, lesbian, or bisexual, these young people shared powerful stories of institutional prejudice that forced each of them to seek refuge at another school. Two had actually dropped out after their schools failed to protect them. They described teachers who would do nothing or even chuckle when other students used words like "faggot" or "dyke" or "queer."

So I should not have been so stunned. School hallways can be a dark place for students. A place that offers no comfort or compassion or sense of connection. Hallways separate. They divide. But for gay/lesbian/bi and questioning youth, high school hallways are especially threatening. Hallways are a battlefield for these students. And rarely do they leave unscarred. They are especially at-risk for substance abuse and school failure. Often alienated from their families, they are at great risk for suicide. With very little support from the schools, these youths travel through their schools afraid.

And nothing is shrouded in darkness more for high school students than issues of sexuality. Students begin their transformation to young adulthood, their bodies change shape and their spirits begin to push and pull and explore. They want to feel power and the effects of their own decisions, seeking independence and autonomy. While teachers demand the mastery of core academic skills, students desire mastery of their social and emotional world. Sexual exploration, through action as well as language, is a way for adolescents to satisfy these developmental demands, but dialogue about sex and issues of sexuality (especially homosexuality) is conspicuously absent from most teachers' curriculums.

Students reflect on sex and sexuality through stories shared from the previous weekend, often embellished to ensure status and power among peers. Students who choose to abstain are silent, left to feel inadequate and self-conscious. The most egregious fate, however, rests with the student unsure of his or her own sexual orientation or those students so sure they openly share their affection with a same-sex partner.

The image of a friend, Katrina, came to mind. We had begun to meet every Friday for coffee or a beer, depending on the week's events. We had developed a friendship outside of school, outside of teaching. She and her partner had welcomed me to their home, we had shared meals, and I felt a strong connection with both these women. I thought of Katrina and felt like a liar.

I looked at my reflection in the window across the hall and saw a person I did not want to recognize. I saw myself with little strength and less integrity to confront what I knew needed redress. The longer I waited the more powerless I felt, and an aching sense of shame spread over me as I walked back to the classroom, past the group of students, silent. I wondered if the private person I thought I was, was actually a sham.

Class began in thirty minutes. I almost walked out of the building and out of teaching. But to continue to teach, I knew I had to share what had happened. I couldn't face the students before I acknowledged the disappointment I felt about the bigotry I had heard in the school—and the disappointment I felt in myself. I sat alone and convinced myself to listen to the students. Explain what happened and let them speak. See how they experience life at the school. Do they know this behavior exists? How do they feel about it? What can I do next time? What can they do?

When I feel nervous before class, I like to move around and speak to students. I like to see what they did over the weekend, talk about their life outside of school, or at least outside of this class. I like to walk around and hear their stories. The movement comforts me and casual conversation before class allows me to slip seamlessly into the teacher role. When students filtered into the room, I began to stroll. I felt conspicuous and stiff.

Somehow I had expected students to already know about what I had heard. I had spent the last forty-five minutes ruminating over it. *Hadn't they*? Of course not. So when a student began to share a story about how a friend's parent had just attended his son's math class, I heard their laughs and wondered whether to purposely create such a difficult situation. I also wondered about the parent in the last class.

When a student's mother walked through the door, I realized it was "switch day." Parents could switch places with their children. I introduced myself to Jason's mother and thanked her for joining us. I didn't explain the day's lesson, but I encouraged her to take part as much as she liked. Jason's mother seemed relaxed. She knew most of the students, and they seemed eager for her to join us.

Jason's mother took a seat, and she looked up with anticipation. Before I had begun to teach, I had imagined an open classroom, where parents felt welcome and attended when they wanted. But now I felt as if my class had become too public, too open. More important, I was concerned the students might censor themselves. Would students feel comfortable discussing homosexuality in front of Jason's mother? Would I?

As usual, Allison was the last to enter. She took her normal seat at the side of the large circle. My voiced cracked, and the students seemed to sense something amiss. I described what I had witnessed. I also described my reaction. They were silent. I closed with, "Do you know this happens in your school? How do you feel about it?" I also shared that I felt as if I had failed as a teacher and asked them, "What can I do next time?" Then I sat back and listened.

A half dozen hands shot up. Many students said they had observed similar incidents at the school. Those who spoke, spoke strongly against the gay bashing they had observed in the school. The class became lively, the room filled with angry voices in dissent of the bigotry. Most teachers want to hear these affirmations from students, but these students seemed to be trying to outdo each other with stories of injustice. The discussion took on a self-righteous and superficial tone.

However, the initial, somewhat contrived, outrage dissipated and another story began to unfold. Two sophomore girls at this semirural school had been holding hands, hugging and kissing in the hallways. Slowly, students began to share how uncomfortable they felt with same-sex affection. Underneath what I had witnessed, then, lay an unacknowledged conflict that students, and probably faculty, had begun to experience but not name.

The morning's incident made more sense. Public display of affection by same-sex partners challenged the school community as it does our larger culture. Students look to each other to make sense of themselves. When they look around and see the range of identities that exist, the sense of their possible selves stretches. When students look into the mirror of each other, they often feel disturbed by what they see. The anxiety may cause some students to lash out and attack those who threaten their fragile sense of who they are.

The conversation turned intimate and personal, more quiet. The students developed a rhythm. They listened to each other share stories. And the stories seemed more real.

Suzanne, an awkward young woman who reads and writes fantasy stories, shared how uncomfortable she felt walking through one particular hall. She said the boys in the hall call her names and tease her. She said she avoids the hall every day and sometimes imagines not coming to school. I asked her if she felt safe at school. She said no. I asked the class how feeling vulnerable in their own school might affect learning.

Students had never discussed safety in school beyond physical safety. But many students began to share stories where they felt vulnerable as they walked around the school or even their towns. Students began to appreciate that a sense of safety extends beyond one's physical well-being.

The stories continued. Two students—one female, the other male—shared stories about relatives who are gay. They both admitted harboring certain prejudices against their relatives until they developed a relationship with them.

Kathleen, the most articulate and serious student in the class, discussed her friendship with her best friend. She and her girlfriend hold hands around town and spend considerable time together. She wondered why she often felt stared at or whispered about when they strolled together, two young women affectionately sharing each other's touch. She said she felt violated at the intrusive questions from her peers who asked about her sexual orientation and wondered about her relationship with her friend.

I was impressed at this story. Kathleen, a very conservative young woman, had emphasized the intrusiveness of others, not the fact that she was heterosexual. She refused to defend her affection for her friend by denying she was a lesbian. So many students, and adults as well, begin a statement with, "I'm not gay or anything, but I totally support gay people." This subtle defense of their heterosexuality through a denial of any homosexual leanings underscores their awareness of the stigma associated with being gay or even acting gay. Defense was not the point or the tone of Kathleen's story. She refused to judge homosexuality; she judged the actions of others who intrude and violate other people's privacy and sense of safety.

The conversation circled back to the two young women. Many students expressed disapproval of same-sex partnerships. They dissented against homosexuality on religious, social, and personal grounds. However, students began to place the issue of bigotry and prejudice in the context of personal safety. Some students began to see how their own prejudices might affect other people's security. And they heard others admit how difficult school was when they felt vulnerable. I shared statistics about gay youth and suicide, hopelessness and school failure.

I thought about the kids from Roots and Branches. I wondered what they might add to this discussion. What would they say to these students? Would they feel comfortable in this classroom? I looked around the room. Students were quiet as they thought about what I had just told them about gay youth. They seemed serious and somewhat taken aback by the level of vulnerability and at-risk potential of gay youth. Would these students listen to the kids from Roots and Branches? Would they mind hearing their stories?

When Allison's hand went up, I immediately called on her. She paused, looked up, and in a shaky voice, said: "You have no idea how hard it is for those girls to show their affection for one another. None of you have any idea how hard it is to come out." She paused. "I'm bisexual," she said, "and whenever I walk around with my girlfriend, I hear the snide comments. I hear what people say. I grew up in a family where that sort of thing was not okay. My family went to church, and being anything but straight was a sin. My father didn't accept it, so I had to go my own way. I made up my mind to live how I wanted to live." She leaned back against her chair and looked out at the class.

The students sat silent. Some started to cry; others started to clap. Many were quiet. The mother looked at me and smiled. Rather than stay silent, Allison had just come out to a room full of people she had barely said a word to the entire year. Allison told us how unsafe she felt in the halls of this school because of her sexual orientation and the harassment she endures because of it. When other students expressed their support, Allison appreciatively said she felt more safe in this classroom than anywhere else in the school.

I remained quiet; the students didn't need me to fill in the spaces, at least not yet. A student had publicly come out in this school, to her classmates. For the first time, Allison took control of her life for that brief moment and held the keys to how she was going to define herself. This is who I am, she said, and I might be petrified to speak the truth but here goes.

I thanked Allison for her courage and the conversation continued. One student questioned how sincere other students' support really was. She thought the support was artificial and wondered what would be said outside the classroom or inside this classroom tomorrow. Another student said she was very proud of the class, but she wondered if everyone was telling the truth or even willing to speak their own truth for fear of reprisal. That was an excellent question, and we talked about how people who disagreed might feel silenced.

I silently surveyed the class. I knew who spoke and who didn't. I wondered about the quiet few. What was simmering in their minds? If they felt silenced, what could I do to encourage their reflection, their understanding? How could they feel free to speak in a way they felt heard while others felt safe? Had I created a climate where some students felt safe to speak at the expense of other students' sense of safety? Did one form of oppression replace another? As teachers, we may have no more difficult task than to teach, respect, and model the inclusion of as many divergent voices as possible, while maintaining the integrity of a safe school environment. As classrooms become more diverse this skill will become even more integral. A safe classroom environment depends on this incredibly demanding mediation.

Many students reflected on how difficult it seemed to make change, especially in a small town where change seemed to happen more slowly. Others encouraged their classmates not to allow the size of the town to dictate how they acted. They demanded that people take responsibility for themselves and not be satisfied with the status quo of their town or school. As class ended, I told the students how proud I was of them. I reminded them that people had shared very intimate experiences. As they left, I encouraged them to look after each other and support one another as they walked through the halls.

I looked at Allison when I said this, and she just smiled. She turned to a friend, and I heard her say, "Man, I was just shaking when I was talking."

But I knew her smiles might end when she walked out of class. Allison had opened herself up and peeled back a part of her guard. And with that exposure comes risk. Allison's coming out would open her to attacks from others who might hear about the discussion. Some students might use this information to justify more bigotry. Classes like this never go unnoticed, and I imagined rumors sweeping through the hallways creating an even more unsafe situation for Allison and other students like her. I knew we needed to support Allison as she confronted the effects of her courage. Leaving the day as finished would be worse than never addressing the bigotry at all. I began to feel the pressure a teacher feels when the lessons merge with students' lives so much so that tests or projects or closing speeches will never end the lesson neatly.

But the lesson never had a chance to end. Melinda and Jenny rushed to me after class. "Some people in this class are hypocrites," Melinda hissed. Jenny nodded intensely, and said: "Just the other day I heard a girl in this class make fun of Allison. And today she says how supportive she is of her." These two young women stared at me, arms folded over their chests and eyes seasoned with spite. They felt the pain that comes from wanting to be part of a community but sensing a false or disingenuous sentiment from some members. Adolescents have a keen sense for hypocrisy. Little shatters the idealism of youth more than hypocrisy.

They, too, may have felt the pain of their silence, as neither addressed this during the discussion. I encouraged them to be patient with other people and reminded them that one conversation won't change everyone, people change at their own pace. I could see the anger and the frustration in their eyes as they accused some classmates of being two-faced. I started to wonder who got the message and who didn't. I began to wonder what the message was.

Jason's mother thanked me before she left. She said the conversation was interesting and wished her son could have been included. She'll never know how much I wanted to sit with her and ask if what had just happened was okay. I needed another adult to process this with. But I imagined her at the next civic function and wondered how long I would last at this school.[1]

The students left the room, and new faces filed in. Through the chaos, I wanted to grab each student before they left and ask how they were doing. I wanted to make sure they were okay. I wanted to know what they thought. When they left, I felt unsure, unable to help feeling like they were more confused or angry or hurt than when they had entered the room. But that's the deal. I've got them for fifty-five minutes every day. Then I watch them leave, unsure of what's really on their minds. Unsure if they like each other or me or even themselves. Then I call roll for twenty-eight fresh faces while the twenty-eight who just left gather for American History.

Like the lesson from that day, Allison's story will never end. She continued to struggle with school, and she experienced bigoted taunts from some students. But Allison began to attend my class. Almost every day. She began to ask questions about the work we were doing. She was much more focused, and her eyes seemed to hold a gaze longer. The gaze was unclouded, alert, present. Allison had begun to awake. She asked for help with her work and occasionally attended the writing center I had started. She asked about her grade, and we discussed how to improve upon last semester's scores.

Every day she attended class, every question she asked, every assignment she completed reinforced what was happening. This young woman had begun to take control of her life. Not without routine struggles of a student or the more intense struggles of this particular adolescent, but Allison had begun to respond and to participate in her education. She began to make positive choices, and she saw the powerful results of these choices.

Why? I think she felt safe in this classroom. She felt listened to and supported. She felt as if she had something to say and that people would listen. This class, and her teacher, would not turn her away because of who she was. She had been alienated from people in the past because of who she was, and in this class, she felt part of a larger community. This community accepted Allison despite what she felt might alienate her from other communities.

Also, she had found an adult ally in the school, someone she trusted. A week after she came out, Allison called me to her desk before class and spoke about a group she had begun attending. She spoke in her normal voice, seemingly unafraid that others might overhear our conversation. She told me she had begun to participate in a gay-friendly youth group outside of school, and she thought I might like to attend sometime.

One adult ally turned into two and two into more. When Allison overheard a bigoted remark directed toward her, she felt safe enough to talk to the school's vice-principal. Instead of withdrawing or passively accepting such attacks, Allison now felt strong enough to tell other adults and ask for support through the normal channels of the school system. She trusted the process to work. It didn't always work, but she began to expect and ask for support instead of isolating herself.

I know Allison will continue to struggle. She'll confront more bigotry in her life, and she'll be challenged in school even with extra help. But as long as Allison and others like her are in school, we as teachers need to attempt to understand their particular needs and respond to these needs. Allison was, and still is, at great risk for school failure. However, because of a safe support system and an environment that allows her to express who she is, Allison has become more committed to school and has changed the course of her education.

The greatest example of Allison's change came during a Coffee Shop Poetry Reading we held in class. Students had been reading and working on poetry and memoir and creative writing—all connected to their sense of place. The last day of the unit, the class contributed to a bagel and doughnut fund, I brought in hot chocolate and tea, and we sat around our classroom-turned-coffee shop and listened to each other read from our portfolios. Allison had worked hard to fulfill the demanding requirements of this project. She met with me after school to discuss Maya Angelou's poem, "The River, the Rock, the Tree." She discovered metaphors and created connections between Maya's imagery and her own sense of place. Allison wrote poetry and completed a discussion of the difficult short story, Charlotte Gilman's "The Yellow Wallpaper."

While other students read, Allison listened attentively. Upon Allison's request, another student read a poem Allison had written. Eventually, Allison asked to read aloud. This young woman, who had been too afraid to venture even a comment throughout much of the year, stepped up to the podium, stood in front of her peers, and read to the class. Other students recognized her strength and the class erupted with cheers.

Teachers have an incredibly difficult and delicate role to play. Life transitions create powerful turmoil for adolescents and need to be addressed as much as the academic challenges that students face. Creating a safe environment for Allison made a tremendous difference for this young woman. Students need to feel as if teachers are there for them, even the students who challenge our own worldview. Often, we as teachers feel passive in the face of conflict, especially concerning such a difficult issue as sexuality. However, our own passivity and powerlessness probably mirror students', and if we can confront and honestly deal with our own darkness, students might learn lifelong lessons from us.

As teachers we need to be aware of the messages we give, the "yes or no, or maybe," that William Stafford (1993) speaks about. Teachers need to give messages to students that say it's okay to speak about things that make them afraid, it's okay to explore their darkness and examine their struggles. But our students will do this only if they feel safe. And we teachers must establish that safety.

Endnote

1 Two weeks later, a group of religious leaders met with the principal to discuss "appropriate educational topics" to be taught at the school. Needless to say, homosexuality did not make the list. Also, two months later, a mother concerned with "how the class was being run" met with me and my mentor. After twenty minutes, she gently asked if this was the class where the lesbian stood up and preached about her gay lifestyle while everyone in the class sat forced into silence by this student's class-long diatribe. I still wonder if this was her daughter's description or how she filled in the blanks of her daughter's story.

Reference

Stafford, William. 1993. A Ritual to Read to Each Other. In Robert Bly, ed., *The Darkness Around Us Is Deep: Selected Poems of William Stafford*, pp. 135–136. New York: HarperPerennial.

13

Talking Like Little Girls: Changing Professional Conversations Among Female Teachers

Brenda Miller Power

EVERY GIRL has her stories. Mine come from fifth grade. That was the year the school district changed the street boundaries for the town in a desperate attempt to even up the number of us baby-boom kids at the different elementary schools in the district. I was moved to a new elementary school, where I knew no one.

At my old school, the girls all played hopscotch during recess. I was a whiz at hopscotch—I could jump through squares as well as any girl. At my new school, all the girls played jump rope. By fifth grade, after years of practice, the ropes were twirling pretty fast, and the chants were very smooth.

I knew nothing about jump rope and all these girls were strangers. For the first week of school I took a book out with me to the playground, squinting in the September sunshine at the pages, with surreptitious glances at the thick gaggle of girls and ropes. My fifth-grade teacher, Mrs. Thompson, came up to me every day and cajoled me to jump rope. Finally, on the last day of the week, she grabbed my hand, made me get up, and said, "C'mon—it's easy. I'll jump with you." She told the girls to slow the ropes down, and she leaped in with me, showing me how to jump to the rhythm. Mrs. Thompson had to be fifty years old, 4′ 10″ and 90 pounds soaking wet. The image of that scrappy teacher, doing whatever she had to do to help her students find friends, is one of the enduring images of my childhood.

But Mrs. Thompson could help only so much. A few weeks later, when one of my classmates had the first birthday slumber party of the year, every single girl in the class was invited—except for me. I got up my courage to ask why I wasn't invited, and the girl patiently explained that there was room in the house for fifteen girls—not sixteen. I cried in the rest room for almost an hour, and Mrs. Thompson was kind enough not to pester me about my tears. What I learned in fifth grade was how hard it is to fit in. At my old school, we played hopscotch, drew, argued over who we'd sit with on the bus. At my new school, all the girls seemed like jump-roping, boy-crazed fools. And I fiercely wanted to be like them. Being a girl suddenly seemed like a mysterious chore.

I'm still here, so the experience didn't kill me. I wish I could say fifth grade was about learning to follow the rules of being a girl, or better yet, learning to break them. But the truth is fifth grade was all about the shock of realizing there *were* rules for being a girl, and somehow I was breaking most of them. Punishment was doled out by my female classmates in subtle and not-so-subtle ways.

I think many girls share my experience of suddenly being on the outside looking in during early adolescence. Though I had moved to a new school, many girls at that age don't need a physical move to find that lifelong girl friends turn away from them. These experiences are so brutal that many of us manage to forget or suppress them. They come back to us when we see our own children or female students struggle at the same age. In my case, the memories flooded back when I read Margaret Atwood's novel *Cat's Eye*. I saw myself and my fifth-grade tormentors in the story of eleven-year-old Elaine, who is alternately taunted and cajoled within her group of friends. As an adult, Elaine watches her daughters closely when they reach the upper elementary grades. She watches and worries:

As my daughters approached this age, the age of nine, I watched them anxiously. I scrutinized their fingers for bites, their feet, the ends of their hair. I asked them leading questions: "Is everything all right, are your friends all right?" And they looked at me as if they had no idea what I was talking about, why I was so anxious. I thought they'd give themselves away somehow: nightmares, moping. But there was nothing I could see, which may only have meant they were good at deception, as good as I was. . . . Most mothers worry when their daughters reach adolescence, but I was the opposite. I relaxed, I sighed with relief. Little girls are cute and small only to adults. To one another they are not cute. They are life-sized. (1989, pp. 105–106)

"*We Want to Be Known*" is written primarily by teachers who work with girls at those pivotal ages of nine to thirteen. The authors watch and worry. In thinking about helping girls of this age, it's important to remember our own experiences in early adolescence. The importance of these memories goes beyond empathy. While we were tormented or tormenting others (on the outside of a group, or protecting our status as insiders), we were learning rules that stay deep within us about how to get along with female peers.

We all want to be Mrs. Thompsons in our professional lives, holding girls by the hand when needed to lead them into new risks and arenas. So much of our talk in schools with female colleagues is rooted in those playground lessons. How we do (and don't) create environments where female teachers can learn and grow together has a direct effect on the ways we think about gender and learning in our own classrooms.

In this essay, I explore patterns of female-to-female talk that have their beginnings on the playgrounds of youth. I focus on two theories of Deborah Tannen—the female ideal of maintaining "common ground" in talk and the value of "rapport talk" over "report talk" among females conversing. These ideas have important implications for professional communities that are primarily female. Finally, I consider ways teachers can break the most harmful and insidious patterns of female-to-female talk, learned in childhood, that inhibit our collaboration with peers.

Standing on Common, Shaky Ground

When teachers I work with read Deborah Tannen's *You Just Don't Understand* (1991) or *Talking 9 to 5: Men and Women in Conversation at Work* (1994), they often share story after story about breakdowns in communication between males and females in their own lives. It's a revelation to all of us to learn the real reasons why men never want to stop at gas stations and ask directions! But while female-male conversation is the central focus of both books, what interests me most in the context of public schools are Tannen's insights into the ways females communicate with each other.

Many elementary and middle schools have large, dominant numbers of women on staff. Even schools that have male instructors often have groups of women who do most of their planning and socializing together. Understanding what gets in the way of change in schools involves understanding how women talk with each other. Women's ways of talking together are filled with unwritten codes, unconscious tight rules of what is shared and what isn't.

For example, Tannen demonstrates how females prefer "rapport" talk to "report" talk. Rapport talk is the chaining of common stories, a hallmark of many teachers' lunchrooms. When someone shares an art lesson disaster that led to paint splattered all over the classroom, another teacher shares a story of Play Doh sculptures made for Mother's Day one year that melted overnight. And so it goes—one story after another to demonstrate implicitly that we all share common ground, we're all in this together, and no teacher is any worse (or any better) than any other teacher in the room. There are many benefits to rapport talk, particularly in building a sense of community and a solid grounding for more intimate advice and support.

In contrast, report talk (a style of talk more often used by men) is the "reporting out" of solutions to any problem presented. Rather than viewing the art lesson disaster as a story to be shared, someone in a "report-talk" mode would view it as a problem to be solved, so that it would never happen again. Someone in a report-talk mode would suggest a different way of doing the lesson. And in doing so, they would unwittingly offend the female teacher who shared the story, who was likely looking for support. Implicitly, rapport talk is viewed by women as opening up and expanding conversation, and report talk is seen as "silencing" or ending the discussion.

The problem with always favoring rapport talk over report talk in schools is that there *are* problems at times that need to be solved. Many of these problems, as any teacher knows, defy any kind of simple pronouncement or solution. But if there is little or no opportunity to move beyond the common ground of sharing stories, there is little opportunity for moving toward solutions to those intractable problems. What's doubly difficult in schools is the very short segments of time teachers have for any talk at all. Ideally, lots of rapport talk eventually can lead to more honest discussion of issues. But in the quick dribs and drabs of conversation available to teachers during the school day, this deep discussion is seldom available.

Consider this fictitious exchange between two teachers in the lunchroom, which echoes conversations teachers tell me about all the time. Lisa is a second-year teacher who has a third-grade class, just beginning a graduate program for certification as a literacy specialist. Jennifer is a twenty-year teaching veteran who completed her specialist degree fifteen years earlier. She works with children in small groups and one-on-one in literacy instruction.

JENNIFER: I was working with Joshua again from your class, Lisa. What a handful he is! As soon I walk away to get a new book, he is bouncing off the walls! I can't believe he's not on Ritalin yet!

LISA: I'm not so sure Ritalin would be the answer for Joshua—it could hurt him more than help him. We were reading an article last week in my graduate course about kids like Joshua. There are a couple of new techniques that may be helpful for him, like providing a different space . . .

JENNIFER [interrupts]: I think I'm pretty current on literacy instruction techniques. I can certainly handle Joshua.

LISA: I wasn't suggesting you aren't current! But if you'd like to read the article I can put a copy in your mailbox.

JENNIFER: Thanks so much, but I think I'll pass.

And then both teachers leave the lunchroom, with small tight smiles on their faces, vaguely at odds with each other. What happened? In order to understand where the conversation breaks down, you need to view it through the lens of Tannen's work. In this expanded transcript, I'll include what was said by Lisa and Jennifer, what was *perceived* by Lisa and Jennifer, and how Tannen's rules were followed or violated:

What was said:	**What was perceived:**	**What Tannen would say:**
JENNIFER: I was working with Joshua again from your class, Lisa. What a handful he is! As soon I walk away to get a new book, he is bouncing off the walls! I can't believe he's not on Ritalin yet!	LISA: Wow! This is exactly what we were talking about in my grad class last week. I don't know Jennifer well, but maybe this is a way for us to connect and talk about literacy and medical issues.	*This is a clear example of Jennifer initiating "rapport talk," the common mode of communication among women. Jennifer doesn't want advice—she just wants support.*

What was said:	**What was perceived:**	**What Tannen would say:**
LISA: I'm not so sure Ritalin would be the answer for Joshua—it could hurt him more than help him. We were reading an article last week in my graduate course about kids like Joshua. There are a couple of new techniques that may be helpful for him, like providing a different space . . .	JENNIFER: Well, isn't this special! It doesn't look like my day's getting any better. Like I'm going to tutored by some young pup I barely know, assigning me reading on problems I've been tackling for twenty years?!	*If Lisa was in a "rapport talk" mode, she would share an anecdote about struggling with Joshua herself, or at least nod sympathetically in support. Instead, she immediately offers advice—a "report talk" style that violates unspoken rules of common ground among women, and so offends Jennifer.*
JENNIFER [interrupts]: I think I'm pretty current on literacy instruction techniques. I can certainly handle Joshua.	LISA: Typical veteran teacher at this school—never open to anything new. At least I try once in a while.	*Because women have so little awareness of the rules that govern their talk, they have little awareness of why communication breaks down.*
LISA: I wasn't suggesting you aren't current! But if you'd like to read the article I can put a copy in your mailbox.	JENNIFER: Oh, yes you were.	*Lessons learned here are negative: Lisa and Jennifer will probably avoid each other, or Lisa has learned never to suggest readings to Jennifer.*
JENNIFER: Thanks so much, but I think I'll pass.		

I'm sure this exchange is painful for Lisa and Jennifer. The breakdown in communication between females at some level always takes us back to the playgrounds of early adolescence, when the rules were new, complex, and seemingly arbitrary. Part of wanting to maintain common ground is a strong, even unconscious desire to remain a part of the group.

The Cat's Eye: Breaking Cultural Patterns

WHEN TEACHERS share common ground at all costs, the cost too often is avoiding different ways of looking at and helping individual students. The first step in breaking through long-held cultural patterns of talk among females is to realize that they *are* cultural. Lisa and Jennifer both might walk away from that exchange blaming themselves for the breakdown, instead of understanding the larger obstacles to open communication.

The central image in Margaret Atwood's *Cat's Eye* (1989) is a cat's eye marble, which the ten-year-old Elaine carries with her as a talisman, hiding it from her friends. In many ways, it represents what is special and unique about Elaine, and what she must keep disguised from her friends so that they won't hurt her. It's a risk for her even to carry the marble with her:

I retrieve my blue cat's eye from where it's been lying all winter in the corner of my bureau drawer. I examine it, holding it up so the sunlight burns through it. The eye part of it, inside its crystal sphere, is so blue, so pure. It's like something frozen in ice. I take it to school with me, in my pocket, but I don't set it up to be shot at. I hold onto it, rolling it between my fingers.

"What's that in your pocket?" says Cordelia.

"Nothing," I say. "It's only a marble."

It's marble season; everyone has marbles in their pockets. Cordelia lets it pass. (p. 128)

What remains frozen in schools at times, carried among individual teachers but hidden from the group, are alternative ways of looking at common problems. These might come from reading teachers have done, from different experiences with the same problems that teachers share. For many teachers, it's too big a risk to defy "rapport talk" styles by presenting new ideas. When teachers like Lisa attempt to break the pattern, they are often rebuffed. The unique, individual solutions needed for helping diverse students can be lost, never spoken within the boundaries of rapport talk.

Tannen's research points to some possibilities for merging the best aspects of rapport and report talk. In my own work with teachers, we have developed a number of strategies that have changed the tenor of talk in small communities of teachers. These changes don't happen overnight, and there is always lots of resistance to disrupting patterns that are comfortable to participants. But these strategies are good starting points for learning to communicate in new ways.

1. *Talk about rapport and report talk.* If possible, do some reading together so that the teachers in your community understand the differences in the terms, and how communication works among males and females.

2. *If you're unsure about the boundaries of the conversation, ask.* Many teachers I work with begin conversations with colleagues with phrases like, "Now, I know you're going to want to give me a solution to my problem, but I'm not looking for that today! I just want a little support!"—a request for rapport talk. Or, "I know you've dealt with problems like the one I'm going to describe. Do you have any suggestions for helping me?"—a request for report talk. In the same vein, if conversation begins to break down, try to step outside the conversation for a moment and think about whether you and the person you are talking with are expecting different things from the conversation. Make these differences a part of the discussion.

3. *Break common ground by identifying the special skills each teacher has in your school.* Every teacher in school has a cat's eye they carry in their pocket—a special skill or expertise that few people know about or acknowledge. A great activity at the beginning of the year or during an inservice day is to put each teacher's name at the center of separate pieces of chart paper and post these pieces of paper around the room. Each teacher then moves around the room, writing

down what special personal or professional skills their colleague has demonstrated during the time they work together. These skills might range from "patient" or "great listener" to "always knows where the missing equipment in the school is!" By identifying and celebrating specialized expertise, the staff prepares itself to accept report talk from knowledgeable individuals during the year when problems arise.

4. *Team teach with female colleagues.* While the structure of some schools doesn't allow for teachers to share their classes completely, there are often opportunities for collaboration around individual projects. Most women need plenty of rapport talk before they are comfortable integrating some report talk into their dialogues. Collaborative work in schools builds in more time, even with students present, for the back-and-forth exchanges that are critical for building trust.

5. *Discuss reading and case studies together*. It's much easier for women to discuss problems together and suggest solutions when the problems aren't housed in their own classrooms. Reading and discussing hypothetical cases encourages teachers, over time, to share similar issues from their own classrooms.

Old Stars and New Light

PART OF the "common ground" many teachers share is a refusal to acknowledge that there are communication problems. Collegiality is prized at the expense of genuine professional collaboration. It's difficult to acknowledge our histories as girls, and how old scars continue to cause new hurts in our relationships with colleagues. At the end of *Cat's Eye*, Elaine has finished thinking about her old relationships with girlfriends, and what they mean for her now:

Now it's full night, clear, moonless and filled with stars, which are not eternal as was once thought. . . . It's old light, and there's not much of it. But it's enough to see by. (pp. 384–385)

We won't have much to go by in breaking patterns of female-to-female talk. The attempts might be awkward, at times hostile, and it will take time.

I suspect there are many girls still who sit alone on playgrounds, hoping for a Mrs. Thompson to take them by the hand and lead them into a game of jump rope with other girls. Perhaps if we can begin to find new ways to fit in and be valued by our adult peers, we'll begin to see alternative ways for the girls in our care to fit in and be valued by their peers. In a world where rapport talk and report talk are both valued by women, it might be possible for that lonely girl just to read her book in peace . . . or even with a nudge from the teacher, to break the routine and show some girls how to play hopscotch.

Female teachers were all once girls, and we have that dim old light to guide us. If we think hard, we can all remember when and where we learned the rules that trap us on common ground, holding onto patterns of talk that don't serve our students (or us) well. It may be old light, but it's good light for understand why professional talk among female teachers is so often unsatisfying, and needs to change.

References

Atwood, Margaret. 1989. *Cat's Eye*. London: Bloomsbury Modern Library.

Tannen, Deborah. 1991. *You Just Don't Understand: Men and Women in Conversation*. New York: William Morrow.

———. 1994. *Talking 9 to 5: Men and Women in Conversation at Work*. New York: William Morrow.

The Tyranny of Nice or Suburban Girl

Sarah J. Liebman

Leave your nice house each morning
and walk nicely down your well-landscaped street.
Wait patiently for the nice yellow bus.
(face behind makeup)

When you arrive at your nice school
you talk nicely with your equally nice friends.
You laugh because you are all wearing the same nice outfit.
(cares behind chitchat)

Then you sit nicely in each class,
listening—but not saying much
and taking notes in your nice handwriting.
"Nice job" reads the red ink on the paper
your nice teacher returned today.
(ideas behind silence)

After school, you go to practice.
Whether you win or lose, you're nice about it.
You get a ride from a nice friend
who drops you off at your nice house
and waves goodbye nicely.
(assertiveness behind a smile)

You sit down to a nice family dinner.
"Did you have a nice day?" they ask.
You nod and everyone talks nicely
but nobody really says anything.
Nicely, you help clean up the kitchen
and then do your homework.
(anything that isn't nice behind anything that is)

"How nice," people say of you.

14

What's a Guy to Do?

Jenny MacMillan

As more and more educators are realizing how significant the middle school years are for shaping gender roles, we are all looking for ways to work with girls in a more positive manner. Besides being a good Spanish teacher, I know that I need to be a good role model for all my students by being outspoken about my beliefs and showing my respect for all people and for different perspectives. But beyond that, as a woman, I can offer something else: I lived through the adolescent-girl culture; I can not only identify with what my middle school girls are going through, but I can see things they aren't aware of. There are dynamics happening in the classroom and in the school culture that the girls often accept as natural. In my role as their teacher, I can adjust my teaching strategies to make sure girls don't fall into a more passive role. I can look at the patterns in their social interactions that are unhealthy and intervene.

My male colleagues don't have this experience to draw on. When I talk with the men I work with, educators I admire, I realize that as they read the literature on adolescent girls, they feel a heightened consciousness about what girls need, but at the same time feel at a loss to change behaviors they can't identify with, and sometimes don't even see. *What's a guy to do?*

As an intern teacher, I noticed that my mentor teacher, Gary Parr, seemed to encourage a welcoming atmosphere for his girl students. It seemed to be a natural for him. But after two lengthy interviews, I found he was quite conscious about his teaching choices and decisions concerning girls. He stressed to me that he makes an effort to treat his students *equitably*—which is different from treating them *equally*. "I try to be consistent in treating all my students on an individual basis," he told me, "which sometimes means making an extra effort to call on girls and make sure their voices are heard."

Gary shared other strategies with me, as have my other male colleagues. The following are some words of wisdom from these men in an attempt to aid other male teachers so they can relate to their girl students in ways that will help them become self-confident, thinking young women.

Tips/Strategies

1. The first step is education. It's important to be aware of the societal pressures on girls and to have resources in the classroom on issues such as: the preoccupation with physical appearance and the unhealthy images of "ideal beauty" our culture promotes, which lead to excessive dieting and even anorexia; pressures to downplay or hide abilities; the need to be liked and to "fit in"—girls' attempts to be agreeable rather than be themselves or challenge the status quo.

Beyond simply being aware of these issues, bring them to your students' attention. For example, if you notice girls "acting dumb" on purpose to get attention from boys, talk with the class as a whole about how behavior such as this can be harmful because it demeans the girl, not to mention reflects negatively on her self-esteem. Students can role-play positive, healthier ways for girls and boys to work together.

2. "It's tempting to compliment girls on appearance and win cheap points," says social studies teacher George Anderson, a veteran of over twenty years. "But I consciously avoid this. Instead, I compliment them on their accomplishments that are related to their work in the class." George recognizes this is hard to do since in our human relationships it feels natural to notice how someone looks or to comment on a new article of clothing. But, he stresses, it's especially important for girls of this age to hear that their male teachers appreciate their ideas over their personal appearance.

3. Teachers should look closely at the content, too, building a fund of materials that supplement the school curriculum. Mark Wandell, a seventh-grade language arts and social studies teacher, brings in material by professional women, such as anthropologists and writers, to make sure his girls recognize the roles women have played in both history and contemporary society. Even in the traditional historical materials that most middle schools use—exploring ancient cultures and emphasizing wars and male-dominated societies—he

encourages his students to look at the parts women played. By comparing women's lives in different cultures and across time, he believes he can help the girls in his class to realize that they have the power in their hands to make changes, not accept things as they exist.

4. Men should be aware of their girl students' "personal space." Gary first brought this to my attention when he told me that he is conscious of his proximity with the girls in his class. For example, one girl who has a history of abuse makes clear through her body language the physical boundaries she has erected around herself. These may be subtle to detect, but it's important for him and other male teachers to honor those boundaries. Other girls, on the other hand, may show that there are times when a quick hug or an arm around the shoulder is appreciated.

It's also important to give girls that extra "space" for their private needs, such as allowing them to leave the classroom if they need to compose themselves, or allowing them to avoid embarrassment if they need to tend to personal hygiene without explanations.

5. One of the ways many young male teachers establish a relationship with their girl students is in a seemingly "harmless" flirtatious relationship. This encourages girls to win approval from men by sexual behavior rather than for the substance of their ideas and their accomplishments. It may feel comfortable and fun to the teacher, but can have long-lasting damaging effects on the girls that are subtle, even subconscious. Instead, male teachers should try to establish relationships with their girl students through encouraging their athletic or artistic interests, fostering extensions in the content the class is exploring together, and helping them develop their own individual talents.

6. Be aware of the messages you send, even in your casual conversation with girls. For example, when you ask your students about their holidays or time out of school, do you have different patterns of questions that are gender-based? Ask a colleague to give you feedback on how you respond to students. You might even audiotape yourself and look closely and critically at your choice of topics and comments.

7. Encourage students to examine the classroom dynamics in terms of gender. Who gets called on? Whose ideas get explored and validated? How do students group themselves?

Teachers can take a proactive role here, too. Forming groups can help promote girls to leadership roles in the class, George believes. "I consider carefully when I form groups, structuring them so that not only will the students be compatible working together, but that stronger boys won't dominate the emerging confidence in the girls."

8. Just as woman can be positive role models for their girl students, men can be positive role models for their boys, and equally important, for their *male colleagues*. Gary's students informed him of a seventh-grade teacher who actually had the girls sit on his lap while he talked with them! The girls told Gary how uncomfortable they felt. Besides addressing it with his whole class, Gary also made a point of calling this man on this behavior. When male colleagues reinforce negative stereotypes for girls, or make comments about their appearance, it's also important to challenge it, rather than ignoring that behavior.

Special thanks to Gary Parr, George Anderson, and Mark Wandell.

15

"It Doesn't Rain Chocolate Chip Cookies": First Steps Toward Change

WE BEGAN this book with the image of a wise woman and a child discovering the secret of wisdom together, looking closely, and wondering how the small things work in the world. It seems fitting to end this collection in the same place. There are many possibilities shown in this book for teachers to work to understand girls. And there are the adolescent girls' voices in these pages, too—alternately funny and poignant as they express what it is like to grow up in American schools. As a reader, you might be wondering how to slow down, look closely, and find your own small starting point for understanding the girls you work with; how to change your practice based on the insights that emerge from your observations. We close this book with some advice from the experts—teachers who have found their own little pieces of classroom life to look at, analyze, and use as a beginning to broaden or change their practice.

Making a Place for Girls

JENNIFER TENDERO and Maureen Barbieri share powerful examples of all-girl groups supported by a teacher. If you are considering starting an all-girl group in your school, it makes sense to find another person who will work with you on the project. Both Jennifer and Maureen relied on colleagues who shared their goals and visions for the groups, and were flexible about adapting those goals and visions as they worked with the girls.

If you do initiate an all-girl discussion or support group in your school, expect some tensions and confrontations with boys or colleagues about the value and purpose of the group. Pat Rawson and Jennifer Baack of Wayne, Maine, decided to start a once-a-week all-girls lunch in their sixth-grade classroom one year when the girls were dramatically outnumbered and outvoiced by the boys in the group (there were twenty boys and six girls in the class). Though the first month of the program went smoothly, the second month brought complaints from the boys that they didn't have their own time with special privileges. The boys were also upset that the girls brought treats from home for the lunches that were shared only among the girls. This led one of the girls to comment in anger, "Boys—they think the sky just rains chocolate chip cookies!" The girls argued that they had taken responsibility for making the lunchtime work.

What followed was a series of healthy and heated discussions in the whole class about the appropriateness of single-sex groups in some instances, the different roles of men and women in society, and the issue of equal voices in the classroom. Pat tape-recorded and analyzed patterns of talk in the classroom throughout the special lunch project, and she found a steady and significant rise in the amount of talk by girls during regular classroom activities throughout the year. In addition, Pat and Jennifer found it was important to include regular surveys and opportunities for written comments from all students. They were surprised at the strong opinions of some of the shy students, male and female, who rarely spoke out in any group setting.

In the end the boys did lobby for and get a few special all-boy lunches, too. Monitored by the male janitor, the boys chose to sit in the classroom in small groups, eating their lunch and watching "The Price Is Right" as their "special time." This wasn't the way the teachers acting alone would have addressed their complaints, but it was a compromise that the students suggested and supported.

Exploring the Subtleties of Talk

For many teachers, understanding girls' place in our society begins with understanding their role in classrooms. Teachers like Jill Ostrow, Ellena Weldon, Sharon Frye, and Jenny MacMillan regularly tape-record and analyze the talk in their classrooms, focusing on points of tension around gender issues when they emerge.

This analysis of talk in the classroom needn't be enormously time-consuming. Peg Welch, a third-grade teacher in Bangor, Maine, regularly tape-records her students and considers gender issues in the classroom. In one discussion of career choices a few years ago, a number of her male students argued that police officers couldn't be women because women weren't strong enough to do the work. This led to a lively exchange about gender roles. In the discussion, Peg did less than 20 percent of the talking. But when she did talk, she nudged students to think more deeply about gender issues with questions like, How many other people believe the statement that was just made about women's strength? Who disagrees? Why do you disagree? At times, a few boys rebelled against the discussion's emphasis on gender. One boy moaned, "Oh no, this class is starting to be just like Oprah!"

Even young boys will confront teachers who engage in "touchy feely" gender discussions. This reflects the culture we live in. Teachers need to be aware of the subtle challenges they will face from both boys and girls as they try to go against the cultural grain when it comes to gender issues. This makes tape-recording and analysis of classroom talk all the more necessary. By considering who talks when, who is left out, and what your own role is as a teacher, you'll have a much better sense over time of how your classroom culture is or isn't changing when it comes to supporting the views and voices of girls.

Tape-recording and analysis can be done without labor-intensive transcribing of tapes. Linda Christensen, a high school teacher in Portland, Oregon, whose female students contributed many pieces to this collection, regularly listens to tapes of students working in small groups as she commutes in her car to work daily. Jennifer Allen, a third-grade teacher in Augusta, Maine, has students listen to and analyze the quality of talk in their peer-led literature discussion groups at least once a week.

Tapes recorded when you are not present are particularly helpful in understanding peer relations. You can listen to these tapes as you respond to student papers or do household chores. As you and your students become more comfortable with tape recorders running all the time, the interactions and analysis of class dynamics will become a more natural and expected process for all.

More Talk About Gender . . . From a Distance

Perhaps the best use of this book with students is the most obvious—the essays and poems from adolescents in this book (such as

"The Tyranny of Nice," "The Wrath of Guess Jeans," or "Tar Baby") are terrific read-alouds for class discussion. When gender issues emerge in classrooms, it can be difficult for students to speak out honestly about them for fear of alienating their peers. If you read the student pieces from this book to your whole class as a way to initiate discussion, girls and boys may find it less threatening to make connections to their own experiences. It's much easier to discuss and consider what another student in another part of the country has experienced as a girl. It's a paradox, but that distance allows for safe talk of more immediate issues. The appendices of this book are filled with books for girls and teachers that can serve a similar purpose—allowing for talk about girls and society in a way that doesn't explicitly condemn the norms of peers.

The wise woman and the young girl end up almost alone at the end of *The Wise Woman and Her Secret*. The crowd of townspeople have left. The two are almost alone—but not quite. They hold between them the start of a relationship built on fascination with and delight in the details of the world. We hope this collection helps you form and develop your own community of teachers and students who care deeply about issues of gender and about making the world a better place for girls. That better world is built slowly, with the small things, one teacher, one girl, one classroom at a time.

Resources

Books for Teachers of Girls

Beyond Dolls and Guns: 101 Ways to Help Children Avoid Gender Bias by Susan Hoy Crawford. 1996. Portsmouth, NH: Heinemann.

A compilation of suggestions and resources for parents and teachers who seek to move beyond gender stereotypes, this little book is essential. The author discusses ways to raise consciousness in classrooms, at home, at play, and in the workplace. She suggests ways to counteract gender bias in the media and in advertising, and she admonishes readers to talk to girls and boys with the same respect and with the same high expectations. The advice is both wise and practical and is bound to generate real thinking.

Beyond Silenced Voices: Class, Race, and Gender in United States Schools edited by Lois Weis and Michelle Fine. 1993. Albany, NY: State University of New York Press.

In these sixteen chapters, we hear from women educators concerned about the personal and political struggles of people who, for various reasons, are often silenced, including women and girls. Carol Gilligan's chapter, "Joining the Resistance," will be particularly relevant.

Failing at Fairness: How Our Schools Cheat Girls by Myra and David Sadker. 1994. New York: Simon and Schuster.

A compilation of more than twenty years of research showing the state of girls' education in America. This book is comprehensive and thought-provoking, making the case for more serious attention to girls' learning at every grade level.

Feisty Females: Inspiring Girls to Think Mathematically by Karen Karp, E. Todd Brown, Linda Allen, and Candy Allen. 1998. Portsmouth, NH: Heinemann.

A rare look at girls and math. The authors show how the use of children's literature featuring "feisty females" facing life head-on with great resourcefulness can help teachers build math confidence in their students.

Girl Power: Young Women Speak Out: Personal Writings from Teenage Girls by Hillary Carlip. 1995. New York: Warner Books.

Hillary Carlip interviewed and corresponded with teenage girls from Los Angeles to Texas to New York, working in inner cities and outlying rural areas. She found that the concerns of girls are the same everywhere, whether they are "homegirls," teen mothers, Native American girls, "farm chicks," "rappers and sistas," or sorority girls. Throughout the book, she shows us how writing has been a powerful force in helping these girls cope with their lives.

Girltalk: All the Stuff Your Sister Never Told You: No Soapboxes, No Sermons, No Nonsense by Carol Weston. 1997. New York: HarperCollins.

Probably the one book no girl between eleven and eighteen should be without, this guide offers a pragmatic, candid, savvy examination of all the issues girls need to consider: bodies, friendship, love, sex, family life, money, education, smoking, drinking, and drugs. The conversational tone is very appealing, and the down-to-earth advice is reassuring for mothers worried about their daughters' decision making. The chapter on appearance and weight control is particularly well done.

Great Books for Girls: More Than 600 Books to Inspire Today's Girls and Tomorrow's Women by Kathleen Odean. 1997. New York: Ballantine.

An annotated list of books featuring strong, brave women and girls, this book is invaluable for teachers and parents. The books are categorized by genre and age level, but the real value is in the author's careful discussion of each title. In her introduction, she tells us that she looked for stories of girls solving problems, girls working well together, mothers encouraging strong traits in their daughters, and women working at a wide variety of jobs. She sought and found folktales that "broke the mold" of the passive-female tale and instead present female protagonists who "confront danger in order to help family or friends." A very useful resource indeed.

In a Different Voice by Carol Gilligan. 1982. Cambridge, MA: Harvard University Press.

In this seminal work, Carol Gilligan presents her widely acclaimed belief that the moral and psychological development of females is unique. This is the book that changes the way we look at girls.

Just Girls: Hidden Literacies and Life in Junior High by Margaret J. Finders. 1997. New York: Teachers College Press.

Margaret Finders's yearlong ethnography of young adolescent girls' informal literacy events provides a rare look at the social lives of the girls, as well as the ways they work through their relationships using literacy as diverse as bathroom graffiti, notes to each other, and reading teen 'zines. The study broadens the view of girls by examining issues of social class as well as gender. Some of Finders's most compelling data lead to a new look at the key role that adult women play in the lives of early adolescent girls.

Making Connections: The Relational Worlds of Adolescent Girls at Emma Willard School edited by Carol Gilligan, Nona P. Lyons, and Trudy J. Hanmer. 1990. Cambridge, MA: Harvard University Press.

Carol Gilligan continues her research on girls' development at Emma Willard School. This book describes the dilemma of girls losing connection with others and risking losing their own voices during adolescence.

Mapping the Moral Domain: A Contribution of Women's Thinking to Psychological Theory and Education edited by Carol Gilligan, Janie Victoria Ward, and Jill McLean Taylor with Betty Bardige. 1988. Cambridge, MA: Harvard University Press.

Fourteen chapters examine girls' issues: relationships, moral development, learning, growing up female in America. Voices of care and justice are carefully examined and explained. A must-read for teachers intrigued by Carol Gilligan's theories of female development.

Meeting at the Crossroads: Women's Psychology and Girls' Development by Lyn Mikel Brown and Carol Gilligan. 1992. Cambridge, MA: Harvard University Press.

This book is the story of Brown and Gilligan's research on girls' moral development at Laurel School in Cleveland, Ohio. It includes case study research over the five-year project and examines girls' decision-making processes, among other moral issues.

Reviving Ophelia: Saving the Selves of Adolescent Girls by Mary Pipher, Ph.D. 1994. New York: Putnam.

A compelling account of the "developmental hurricane" no young woman escapes, this book offers explanations for why girls change and struggle through adolescence and offers suggestions for what the adults in their lives might do to help them cope and survive.

SchoolGirls: Young Women, Self-Esteem, and the Confidence Gap by Peggy Orenstein. 1994. New York: Doubleday.

A journalist's look at the behind the scenes lives of adolescent girls, this book raises huge concerns about girls' loss of self-esteem at a precarious time in their lives. A page turner written in snappy, conversational style, this book is one readers will not be able to put down.

A Sense of Self: Listening to Homeschooled Adolescent Girls by Susannah Sheffer. 1995. Portsmouth, NH: Boynton Cook/Heinemann.

A close-up look at girls who are managing to safeguard their strong voices, their self-confidence, and their courage, Sheffer's book presents another view of what girls need. Surprising, moving, and well worth reading.

Sounds from the Heart: Learning to Listen to Girls by Maureen Barbieri. 1995. Portsmouth, NH: Heinemann.

Stories from one seventh-grade classroom show girls' struggles and a teacher's attempt to help them speak out.

Weaving in the Women: Transforming the High School English Curriculum by Liz Whaley and Liz Dodge. 1993. Portsmouth, NH: Boynton Cook/ Heinemann.

Arguing that it is vital for girls to read works by and about women, Whaley and Dodge present a compelling argument for changing the traditional literature curriculum. Their book offers lists of resources as well as comprehensive suggestions for how to present these works to students. Even though they deal with high school curriculum, this book will be a great eye-opener for middle school teachers as well.

You've Got To Read This! Recommendations by Girls, for Girls

Megan Hochstetler, Riverdale High School, recommends:

Kindred by Octiva Buttler. Garden City, NY: Doubleday. 1979.

What would you say if you suddenly were zapped back in time to the antebellum South to help a young white boy who is in actuality your ancestor?

You would probably be scared out of your skin, especially if you were like Dana, a black woman who must save her ancestor from himself. She must be sure a young black girl named Alice, and this boy, Rufus, conceive a baby girl who is to be Dana's great-great-grandmother. *Kindred* is a roller-coaster ride of emotions, ranging from wanting to kill some of the characters to feeling the pain of a whip on your very own back. This is a wonderful book for all ages, full of the determination within the human spirit.

To Kill a Mockingbird by Harper Lee. Philadelphia: Lippincott. 1960.

What an unimaginably difficult life to lead for a young girl like Scout. No mother, a fifty-year-old or so father, a housekeeper who is always getting on her nerves, her one friend—besides her brother—a boy, and a phantom of a neighbor who lives just two doors from her home. Through all of this and the "storm" that is brewing in the city of Maycomb, she makes everything seem absolutely simple. Reading through the eyes of a nine-year-old child is definitely a refreshing experience. Through Harper Lee's short powerful sentences, mystery, suspense, and the determined and innocent spirit of a child shines brightly in this masterpiece.

Juniper by Monica Furlong. New York: Knopf, distributed by Random House. 1991.

Ninnoc can definitely be called a child of wealth; always wanting her way, and always getting it. The heir to her father's throne, she is sent to live with her godmother Euny, a doran (sorceress) in the forest. Euny is hard and cruel, but she teaches Ninnoc how to be a doran. On her journey of learning the doran ways and spells, Ninnoc learns more about herself. Becoming "Juniper" as the stars said she would the day she was born, she must stop her evil aunt from hurting her unborn baby brother and the rest of her family. This book is an exciting adventure that takes the reader through mysterious lands of old. Enchantment runs wild through this wonderful book and *Wise Child,* the first book in the Juniper series.

White Lilacs by Carolyn Meyer. New York: Harcourt Brace. 1993.

Rose Lee's family is strong and upbeat. They live in Freedomtown, Freedom for short, in the middle of the city of Dillon. All of the black folks in town live in Freedom—Grandpa Jim and Grandma Lila, Nancy Lee, Lora Lee, and Henry. Rose Lee loves her friends and family in Freedom. Then the white folks in the city of Dillon tell all the residents in Freedom that they need to get out and move to a place outside of Dillon called the Flats so that the city can build a park where Freedom stands! The people who live in Freedom are infuriated and little Rose Lee finds herself in the middle of the debate about how to respond to the city. *White Lilacs* is a pure, sweet book about an unfair event in an angelic child's life. This book captivates the happiness and sorrow in a child's soul.

Shizuko's Daughter by Kyoko Mori. New York: Holt. 1993.

Yuki was a very active girl. She did sports, was a wonderful student, always happy around her friends, and president of her school's student council. What a perfect life, right? Well, it seems that way but Yuki is hiding a dark secret. "Be good. You know I love you." These were the last words Shizuko, Yuki's mother, had said before Yuki came home and found her mother was dead. Shizuko had killed herself, and now Yuki must find a way to go on with her uncaring father and horrible stepmother. This detailed novel is scarcely unemotional and moving. You'll cry, you'll laugh, you'll understand the life of a motherless child. Of any book, this is the one you must read.

Sarah J. Liebman and Ursula A. Whitcher, Lake Oswego High School, recommend:

Ain't I a Woman: A Book of Women's Poetry from Around the World edited by Illona Linthwaite. New York: Wings Books. 1987.

This anthology contains the poetry of women of many backgrounds. We especially recommend "Growing Up," "Witch," "The House of Desire," "They Went Home," and "Eve Meets Medussa." The poets range from Sappho, Sojourner Truth, Alice Walker, Marge Piercy, Maya Angelou, and Gabriela Mistral to twelve-year-old Zindziswa Mandela.

"Our Changing Sense of Self." *Our Bodies, Ourselves: A Book by and for Women* by the Boston Women's Health Collective. New York: Simon and Schuster. 1973.

We highly recommend this chapter, which discusses becoming more integrated human beings, changing values, rediscovering activity, rediscovering anger, and seeking independence. We disagree on the rest of the book. Perhaps some of the newer books aimed at girls in this age group would be better for the medical information, which some of us think is out of date. This book is great because of its feminist perspective.

Homecoming. 1981; *Dicey's Song*. 1983; *A Solitary Blue*. 1983; and *Seventeen Against the Dealer*. 1989 by Cynthia Voigt. New York: Atheneum.

In *Homecoming*, Dicey Tillerman and her younger brothers and sisters are deserted in a mall by their beautiful, fragile mother. Dicey must take them to live with their grandmother. They walk to Maine from Connecticut. In Newbury Award-winning *Dicey's Song*, the children have arrived in Maine but the family's troubles are not over. Dicey and her grandmother are brave, strong, smart, independent, and determined. Dicey meets Jeff, the main character of *A Solitary Blue*. Jeff is a sensitive protagonist with whom the reader can empathize. Throughout these books the Tillermans remain devoted to each other. Although I greatly admired Dicey, I found *Homecoming* very disturbing. *Dicey's Song* is moving and deserves the Newbury Award it won. *A Solitary Blue* is also a beautiful book. In *Seventeen Against the Dealer*, Dicey and the Tillermans continue to shine as seventeen-year-old Dicey encounters adversity in starting her own business constructing boats.

Pageant by Katheryn Lasky. New York: Four Winds. 1986.

The protagonist in this novel is strong, intelligent, and authentic, as are her mother and sister. The book describes the coming of age of a Jewish girl attending a Catholic School. Year after year she plays a shepherd in the Christmas pageant while the pretty girls play angels. She copes with her hypercritical aunt moving in, her sister's departure for college, her high school, her own attitudes toward sex, and the tumult of the Kennedy assassination. Easy to relate to, this novel is remarkable for the honesty with which it portrays its characters and their lives.

Enchanter's Glass by Susan Whitcher. San Diego: Jane Yolen Books, Harcourt Brace. 1996.

This work is an allegory about a girl named Phoebe based on Spenser's *Fairie Queen*. Phoebe's best friend has discovered makeup and boys while Phoebe is trying to figure out when adult human beings are allowed to use imagination. Her father is basically fading out of consciousness. Her mother is a hyperworried concert violist. The story starts when Phoebe skips school. She's standing on the bridge over the river by her house, and life suddenly feels very worthless; she falls in. In the river, she finds a shard of glass. If she looks through it, things are different: her neighbor is an evil enchanter, her father simply isn't there. Then Phoebe finds the class outcast in her backyard. He's wearing her father's Hawaiian shirt. He's half goat.

Alanna: The First Adventure. 1989; *In the Hand of the Goddess*. 1990; *The Woman Who Rides Like a Man*. 1990; and *Lioness Rampant* 1988 by Tamora Pierce. New York: Random House.

These are not the most well-crafted books, but the series does have a very strong heroine. Alanna pretends to be a boy so that she can become a knight, and becomes one of the best in the realm, but then she has to deal with the fact that she's a woman, too. We loved these books.

Witch Week by Diana Wynne Jones. New York: Greenwillow. 1993.

In an alternate England where witches are still burned, a boarding-school class gets a note: "Somebody in this room is a witch." One of the main characters is Nan, a rather chubby, hopeless girl who finds herself becoming a witch (and a writer). This novel is Ursula's sister's favorite. Jones also wrote *The Lives of Christopher Chant, Fire and Hemlock,* and many other novels. We would recommend Diana Wynne Jones in general because her books are very funny without sacrificing ideas.

Sarah J. Liebman and Hannah Druckman, Lake Oswego High School, recommend:

The Mozart Season by Virginia E. Wolff. New York: Holt. 1991.

Allegra Shapiro is selected to participate in a prestigious music competition. She spends a summer learning about life and music. She makes peace with the Holocaust, befriends a dancing stranger and a heartbroken vocal soloist, and comes to understand the nature of art. She, her teacher, her family, and a family friend who visits are all well-drawn characters. This novel is exceptional for its sensitivity. The realizations are lovely and the reader reaches them together with Allegra.

Books for Girls

Nonfiction Books Addressing Contemporary Girls' Concerns

Girls Speak Out: Finding Your True Self by Andrea Johnston. 1997. New York: Scholastic.

The author speaks directly to young readers from nine to fourteen about self-esteem and about girls' groups across the country that celebrate and strengthen bonds among girls by looking at historical rituals and traditions and examining their value in today's world. The importance of women's relationships with girls is emphasized.

Girltalk: All the Stuff Your Sister Never Told You: No Soapboxes, No Sermons, No Nonsense by Carol Weston. 1997. New York: HarperCollins.

Breezy, pragmatic, comforting book about the biggest issues on girls' minds: bodies, relationships, self-confidence, the future for women. The chapters addressing appearance and weight are particularly strong. This book should be required reading for girls between eleven and sixteen.

It's a Girl Thing: How to Stay Healthy, Safe, and in Charge by Mavis Jukes. 1996. New York: Knopf.

Practical guide offering information on girls' changing bodies and feelings. The author writes with common sense and a wonderful sense of humor, resulting in a tone that is refreshing, credible, and reassuring.

Totally Private and Personal: Journaling Ideas for Girls and Young Women by Jessica Walter. 1996. Minneapolis, MN: Free Spirit.

Written by a teenage girl, this book offers specific suggestions for journal writing for girls. The author offers tips for using writing to examine changing lives, using her own experiences and opinions as examples. Great suggestions for books to read are interspersed with writing invitations. Younger girls (nine to twelve) will find this book particularly appealing.

Books Starring Girls and Women

Most of what girls read in schools is written by men about men. We need more stories of women who are strong, more examples of women in a variety of roles. . . . Girls need to see reflections of themselves in all their diversity—as workers, artists, and explorers.

MARY PIPHER, *Reviving Ophelia*

Aikath-Gyaltsen, Indrani. 1991. *Daughters of the House.* New York: Ballantine.
Alexander, Lloyd. 1990. *The Illyrian Adventure.* New York: Bantam Doubleday.
Angelou, Maya. 1969. *I Know Why the Caged Bird Sings.* New York: Random House.
Angell, Jude. 1990a. *Don't Rent My Room.* New York: Bantam.
———. 1990b. *Leave the Cooking to Me.* New York: Bantam.
Anonymous. 1972. *Go Ask Alice.* New York: Avon.
Armstrong, Jennifer. 1993. *Steal Away.* New York: Scholastic.
Atwood, Margaret. 1986. *The Handmaid's Tale.* Boston: Houghton Mifflin.
———. 1989. *Cat's Eye.* London: Bloomsbury Modern Library.
Avi. 1990. *The True Confessions of Charlotte Doyle.* New York: Avon.
Berg, Elizabeth. 1993. *Durable Goods.* New York: Random House.
Betancourt, Jeanne. 1991. *More Than Meets the Eye.* New York: Bantam Doubleday.
Calvert, Pat. 1992. *When Morning Comes.* New York: Avon.
Cather, Willa. [1918] 1994a. *My Antonia.* New York: Signet.
———. [1913] 1994b. *O Pioneers.* New York: Penguin.
Cisneros, Sandra. 1991. *The House on Mango Street.* New York: Random House.
———. 1992. *Woman Hollering Creek.* New York: Random House.
Clapp, Patricia. 1988. *Tamarack Tree.* New York: Puffin.
Cole, Brock. 1991. *Celine.* New York: Farrar, Straus, and Giroux.
———. 1992. *The Goats.* New York: Farrar, Straus, and Giroux.
Collier, James, and Christopher Collier. 1984. *Who Is Carrie?* New York: Dell.
———. 1991. *War Comes to Willy Freeman.* New York: Dell Delacorte.
Conrad, Pam. 1987. *Prairie Songs.* New York: HarperCollins.
Crew, Linda. 1989. *Children of the River.* New York: Dell.
———. 1995. *Fire on the Wind.* New York: Dell Delacorte.
Cushman, Karen. 1995a. *Catherine, Called Birdy.* New York: HarperTrophy.
———. 1995b. *The Midwife's Apprentice.* Boston: Clarion.
Daly, Maureen. 1986. *Acts of Love.* New York: Scholastic.

Danziger, Paula. 1979. *The Cat Ate My Gymsuit*. New York: Dell.
———. 1983. *The Divorce Express*. New York: Dell.
DePau, Linda Grant. 1975. *Founding Mothers: Women of America in the Revolutionary Era*. Boston: Houghton Mifflin.
Derby, Pat. 1989. *Goodbye, Emily, Hello*. New York: Farrar, Straus, and Giroux.
Dickinson, Peter. 1990. *Eva*. New York: Dell.
———. 1995. *A Bone from the Dry Sea*. New York: Dell.
Dillard, Annie. 1988. *An American Childhood*. New York: HarperCollins.
———. 1990. *The Writing Life*. New York: HarperCollins.
Dorris, Michael. 1988. *A Yellow Raft in Blue Water*. New York: Warner.
Duford, Deborah, and Harry S. Stout. 1987. *An Enemy Among Them*. Boston: Houghton Mifflin.
Duncan, Lois. 1982. *Chapters: My Growth as a Writer*. Boston: Little, Brown.
———. 1989. *Stranger with My Face*. Boston: Little, Brown.
Fox, Paula. 1988. *The Moonlight Man*. New York: Dell.
Frank, Anne. 1952. *The Diary of a Young Girl*. Garden City, NY: Doubleday.
Furlong, Monica. 1989. *Wise Child*. New York: Random House.
———. 1991. *Juniper*. New York: Knopf, distributed by Random House.
Garden, Nancy. 1982. *Annie on My Mind*. New York: HarperCollins.
George, Jean C. 1974. *Julie of the Wolves*. Madison, WI: Demco Media.
Grealy, Lucy. 1994. *Autobiography of a Face*. Boston: Houghton Mifflin.
Greene, Bette. 1973. *Summer of My German Soldier*. New York: Dial.
———. 1992. *The Drowning of Stephen Jones*. New York: Dell.
Griffin, Peni R. 1993. *Switching Well*. New York: Margaret K. McElderry.
Guy, Rosa. 1983. *The Friends*. New York: Bantam Books.
Hahn, Mary. 1988. *December Stillness*. Boston: Clarion.
Hamilton, Morse. 1990. *Effie's House*. New York: Greenwillow.
Hamilton, Virginia. 1990. *Cousins*. New York: Philomel.
———. 1995. *Her Stories: African-American Folktales, Fairy Tales, and True Tales*. New York: Scholastic.
Hayden, Torey. 1980. *One Child*. New York: Putnam.
———. 1989. *Just Another Kid*. New York: Avon.
———. 1995. *The Tiger's Child*. New York: Scribner.
Hendrey, Francis. 1990. *Quest for a Maid*. New York: Farrar, Straus, and Giroux.

Herlihy, Dirlie. 1988. *Ludie's Song*. New York: Dial Books for Young Readers.

Hesse, Karen. 1992. *Letters from Rifka*. New York: Holt.

———. 1994. *Phoenix Rising*. New York: Holt.

Higginsen, Vy. 1992. *Mama, I Want to Sing*. New York: Scholastic.

Hoffman, Alice. 1989. *At Risk*. New York: Berkley.

———. 1990. *Seventh Heaven*. New York: Putnam.

———. 1995. *Practical Magic*. New York: Putnam.

Howard, Ellen. 1988. *Her Own Song*. New York: Atheneum.

Hurmence, Belinda. 1984. *Tancy*. Boston: Clarion.

Hurston, Zora Neale. 1937. *Their Eyes Were Watching God*. Urbana, IL: University of Illinois Press.

Idilbi, Ulfat. 1995. *Sabriya: Damascus Bitter Street*. Brooklyn, NY: Interlink.

Irwin, Hadley. 1991. *What About Grandma?* New York: Avon.

Johnson, Angela. 1993. *Toning the Sweep*. Custer, WA: Orca.

Johnston, Norma. 1988. *The Potter's Wheel*. Boston: Morrow Junior Books.

Kaye, Marilyn. 1987. *Lydia*. New York: Harcourt Brace.

Keehn, Sally. 1991. *I Am Regina*. New York: Philomel.

Kincaid, Jamaica. 1986. *Annie John*. New York: New American Library.

———. 1990. *Lucy*. New York: Farrar, Straus, Giroux.

Kingston, Maxine Hong. 1975. *The Woman Warrior: Memoirs of a Girlhood Among the Ghosts*. New York: Knopf.

Lasky, Kathryn. 1986a. *Night Journey*. Madison, WI: Demco Media.

———. 1986b. *Pageant*. New York: Four Winds.

Levy, Marilyn. 1996. *Run for Your Life*. Boston: Houghton Mifflin.

Lindgren, Astrid. 1981. *Ronia, the Robber's Daughter*. New York: Puffin.

Lowry, Lois. 1987. *Rabble Starkey*. Boston: Houghton Mifflin.

———. 1989. *Number the Stars*. Boston: Houghton Mifflin.

———. 1991. *Anastasia at This Address*. Boston: Houghton Mifflin.

Lunn, Janet. 1983. *The Root Cellar*. New York: Puffin.

MacLachlan, Patricia. 1990. *The Facts and Fictions of Minna Pratt*. New York: Harper and Row.

Mark, Jan. 1983. *Handles*. New York: Atheneum.

Markandaya, Kamala. 1990. *Nectar in a Sieve*. Madison, WI: Demco Media.

Mazer, Harry. 1991. *The Island Keeper*. Madison, WI: Demco Media.

Mazer, Norma Fox. 1973. *A Figure of Speech*. New York: Delacorte.

———. 1984. *Mrs. Fish, Ape, and Me, the Dump Queen*. New York: Avon.

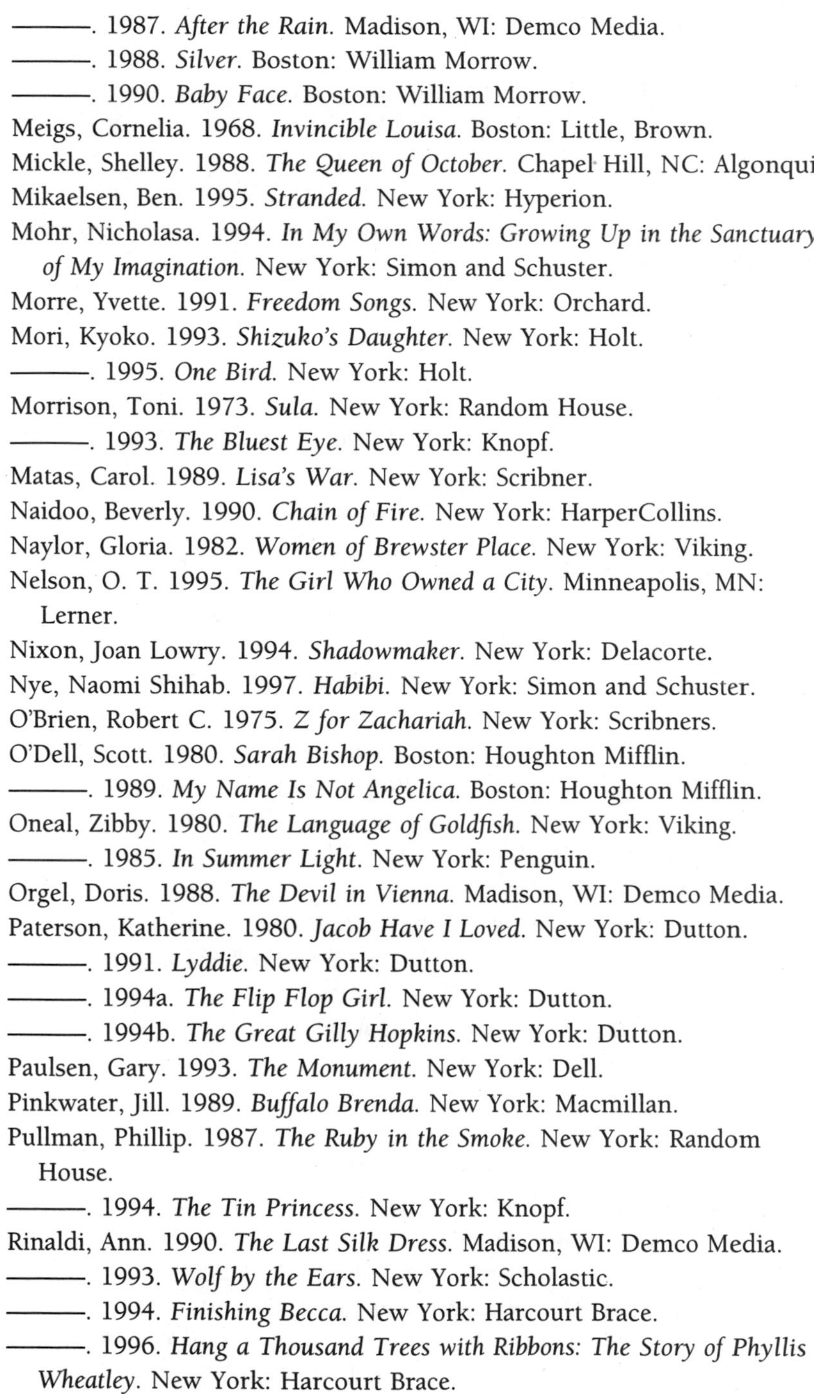

———. 1987. *After the Rain*. Madison, WI: Demco Media.
———. 1988. *Silver*. Boston: William Morrow.
———. 1990. *Baby Face*. Boston: William Morrow.
Meigs, Cornelia. 1968. *Invincible Louisa*. Boston: Little, Brown.
Mickle, Shelley. 1988. *The Queen of October*. Chapel Hill, NC: Algonquin.
Mikaelsen, Ben. 1995. *Stranded*. New York: Hyperion.
Mohr, Nicholasa. 1994. *In My Own Words: Growing Up in the Sanctuary of My Imagination*. New York: Simon and Schuster.
Morre, Yvette. 1991. *Freedom Songs*. New York: Orchard.
Mori, Kyoko. 1993. *Shizuko's Daughter*. New York: Holt.
———. 1995. *One Bird*. New York: Holt.
Morrison, Toni. 1973. *Sula*. New York: Random House.
———. 1993. *The Bluest Eye*. New York: Knopf.
Matas, Carol. 1989. *Lisa's War*. New York: Scribner.
Naidoo, Beverly. 1990. *Chain of Fire*. New York: HarperCollins.
Naylor, Gloria. 1982. *Women of Brewster Place*. New York: Viking.
Nelson, O. T. 1995. *The Girl Who Owned a City*. Minneapolis, MN: Lerner.
Nixon, Joan Lowry. 1994. *Shadowmaker*. New York: Delacorte.
Nye, Naomi Shihab. 1997. *Habibi*. New York: Simon and Schuster.
O'Brien, Robert C. 1975. *Z for Zachariah*. New York: Scribners.
O'Dell, Scott. 1980. *Sarah Bishop*. Boston: Houghton Mifflin.
———. 1989. *My Name Is Not Angelica*. Boston: Houghton Mifflin.
Oneal, Zibby. 1980. *The Language of Goldfish*. New York: Viking.
———. 1985. *In Summer Light*. New York: Penguin.
Orgel, Doris. 1988. *The Devil in Vienna*. Madison, WI: Demco Media.
Paterson, Katherine. 1980. *Jacob Have I Loved*. New York: Dutton.
———. 1991. *Lyddie*. New York: Dutton.
———. 1994a. *The Flip Flop Girl*. New York: Dutton.
———. 1994b. *The Great Gilly Hopkins*. New York: Dutton.
Paulsen, Gary. 1993. *The Monument*. New York: Dell.
Pinkwater, Jill. 1989. *Buffalo Brenda*. New York: Macmillan.
Pullman, Phillip. 1987. *The Ruby in the Smoke*. New York: Random House.
———. 1994. *The Tin Princess*. New York: Knopf.
Rinaldi, Ann. 1990. *The Last Silk Dress*. Madison, WI: Demco Media.
———. 1993. *Wolf by the Ears*. New York: Scholastic.
———. 1994. *Finishing Becca*. New York: Harcourt Brace.
———. 1996. *Hang a Thousand Trees with Ribbons: The Story of Phyllis Wheatley*. New York: Harcourt Brace.

Roth-Hano, Renee. 1988. *Touch Wood: A Girlhood in Occupied France.* New York: Four Winds.
Rylant, Cynthia. 1989. *But I'll Be Back Again: An Album.* New York: Orchard.
———. 1990. *A Couple of Kooks and Other Stories About Love.* New York: Orchard.
Sebestyn, Ouida. 1988. *The Girl in the Box.* Boston: Little Brown.
Sinclair, April. 1995. *Coffee Will Make You Black.* New York: Avon.
Smith, Betty. 1943. *A Tree Grows in Brooklyn.* New York: Harper Brothers.
Snyder, Zilpher K. 1990. *Libby on Wednesday.* New York: Bantam.
Speare, Elizabeth. 1958. *The Witch of Blackbird Pond.* Boston: Houghton Mifflin.
Spinelli, Jerry. 1991. *There's a Girl in My Hammerlock.* New York: Simon and Schuster.
Staples, Suzanne F. 1989. *Shabanu: Daughter of the Wind.* New York: Random House.
———. 1993. *Haveli.* New York: Knopf.
Sullivan, Faith. 1988. *The Cape Ann.* New York: Crown.
Tan, Amy. 1995. *The Hundred Secret Senses.* New York: Ballantine.
Taylor, Mildred D. 1976. *Roll of Thunder, Hear My Cry.* New York: Dial.
Temple, Francis. 1995. *Tonight, by Sea.* New York: Orchard
Thesman, Jean. 1990. *Rachel Chance.* Boston: Houghton Mifflin.
———. 1991. *The Rain Catchers.* Boston: Houghton Mifflin.
Townsend, Sue. 1987. *The Secret Diary of Adrian Mole, Aged 13¾.* Madison, WI: Demco Media.
Voigt, Cynthia. 1981. *Homecoming.* New York: Atheneum.
———. 1982. *Tell Me if Lovers Are Losers.* New York: Atheneum.
———. 1983. *Dicey's Song.* New York: Atheneum.
———. 1985. *Jackaroo.* New York: Atheneum.
———. 1986. *Come a Stranger.* New York: Atheneum.
———. 1990. *On Fortune's Wheel.* New York: Atheneum.
———. 1996. *The Bad Girls.* New York: Scholastic.
Walker, Alice. 1982. *The Color Purple.* New York: G. K. Hall.
Wallace, Bill. 1993. *Never Say Quit.* New York: Holiday House.
Wallis, Velma. 1993. *Two Old Women.* Seattle, WA: Epicenter.
Walsh, Jill Patton. 1969. *Fireweed.* Columbus, OH: Macmillan.
Welty, Eudora. 1985. *One Writer's Beginnings.* New York: G. K. Hall.
Wilson, Budge. 1992. *The Leaving and Other Stories.* New York: Putnam.
Wolff, Virginia E. 1991. *The Mozart Season.* New York: Holt.

Yamanaka, Lois-Ann. 1996. *Wild Meat and the Bully Burgers*. New York: Farrar, Straus, and Giroux.
Yep, Laurence. 1977. *Child of the Owl*. New York: HarperCrest.
———. 1996. *Ribbons*. New York: Putnam.

Contributors

The morning he finished this project, *Steve Brand* convinced himself to accept his first full-time teaching job as a seventh- and eighth-grade humanities teacher at a small school nestled under the western shadow of Mt. Hood in Welches, Oregon. As much as he loves his home on the Sandy River, some days he wishes revisions had lasted just one week longer. But he always encourages students to write from the stories they carry within.

Since *Tera Cushman* has lived only fifteen years on this planet (no comment about any other one), she has not done much that has enough significance to be mentioned here. She has lived thirteen of those fifteen years in Portland, Oregon. The other two were spent in Texas (or so she's told), where she was born. She is currently a freshman (help!) at Catlin Gabel High School in the class of '01. Since there isn't much else to say, she'd like to take this opportunity to thank the Academy, her mom, her dad, every last one of her fanatical relatives, and . . . okay, she'll stop now.

Sharon Frye teaches integrated English/history classes at Riverdale High School in Portland, Oregon. She is in her second year of teaching and finds working with adolescents invigorating, challenging, and rewarding. However, she is also looking forward to a vacation with a pile of books in a warm and sunny place.

A former elementary school teacher, *Karen Karp* is an associate professor of mathematics education at the University of Louisville. The focus of her work is on helping girls to be more successful in mathematics. Her recent publication *Feisty Females: Inspiring Girls to Think Mathematically* (1998) examines ways to link mathematics instruction to children's literature about strong female characters.

Stan Karp teaches high school English and journalism in Paterson, New Jersey. He is an editor of the urban educational journal *Rethink-*

ing Schools and co-chair of the National Coalition of Education Activists.

Jenny MacMillan teaches Spanish to middle school kids in Beaverton, Oregon. Meeting monthly with a small group of teacher researchers, she is able to address and discuss gender issues with others who have a similar interest and concern about the direction in which many middle school-aged girls are headed.

Jill Ostrow has spent the last seventeen years teaching children and teachers. Her book *A Room with a Different View* (1995) focuses on the experiences she had with one of her 1-3 multiage classrooms. Her new book, *Making Problems, Creating Solutions* (1998), talks about the discoveries she has made in mathematical thinking. Jill is currently taking on a new challenge: she is teaching at Lewis and Clark College in the teacher education department working with pre-service elementary teachers.

Kiran Dilip Purohit has been a new science teacher and a new New Yorker for two years; she teaches in Chinatown.

Jennifer DeGraaf Tendero teaches seventh-grade English and social studies in the Bronx, New York, and lives in Brooklyn with her husband, Antonio Tendero. She has recently completed her M.A. in English education from Columbia University Teachers College.

Ellena Weldon has been teaching high school and middle school Spanish and English for the past two years in Portland, Oregon. Before becoming a teacher she attended various educational institutions in Stockton, California, Honolulu, Hawaii, and Portland, Oregon. She continues to conduct classroom research related to literacy and gender. She also maintains the habit of keeping a diary, but does not intend to publish her current entries any time soon.